VANISHING ENGLAND

A PHOTOGRAPHIC JOURNEY

THROUGH ENGLAND'S THREATENED LANDSCAPES

Text by
 GARETH HUW DAVIES
Introduction by
 JOHN LE CARRÉ
Photographs by
 HEATHER ANGEL
 CLIVE ARROWSMITH
 DAVID BAILEY
 JOHN BLAKEMORE
 PETER CATTRELL
 JOHN DAVIES
 TERENCE DONOVAN
 FAY GODWIN
 GRAEME HARRIS
 HELEN HARRIS
 CHRISTOPHER JOYCE
 STEPHEN LAWSON
 PATRICK LICHFIELD
 JENNY MAY
 LINDA McCARTNEY
 DONALD McCULLIN
 GARRY MILLER
 ALISTAIR MORRISON
 CRESSIDA PEMBERTON-PIGOTT
 SNOWDON
 KOO STARK
 PAUL WAKEFIELD
 DENIS WAUGH
 MICHAEL WESTMORELAND

VANISHING ENGLAND

A PHOTOGRAPHIC JOURNEY

THROUGH ENGLAND'S THREATENED LANDSCAPES

SALEM HOUSE PUBLISHERS
TOPSFIELD, MASSACHUSETTS

Contents

PAGES 1 TO 5 *The view from Honey Hill, Northamptonshire, showing the route of the proposed A1-M1 motorway link-road (Photo: Michael Westmoreland)*

Introduction

JOHN LE CARRÉ

It is a gorgeous English autumn morning and we have driven through some of the loveliest countryside I have seen in my life, anywhere in the world: from Newbury, through the Bourne Valley, into the wilds of central Dorset. Mrs Bridges starts talking as soon as we sit down. The intensity was in her before we arrived, and it will surely remain after we have gone. She talks from the kitchen. She talks while she stands with her back to us, pointing out things on the battle-map that hangs, hand-covered in cellophane, on the dining-room wall. Her subject is The Threat. She is small and greying and quick. She teaches music, mainly to children, and she loves nature. Look at the gramophone records and tapes on the shelves. Look at the sunlight bathing the fields outside the window. She is a woman of obvious and uncomplicated decency and she has the urgent dediction you find in people who run youth clubs in bad areas, or work in the remoter kibbutzim. Four cooling towers at least, she says, talking to the map – but ask my husband, he knows more about it. Three hundred and sixty foot high and roughly as wide at the base, each one of them. Just up there on the heath, she says, my husband will take you up and show you. She offers us coffee, she talks about the heath's association with Thomas Hardy and the composer Holst, she fetches a volume of John Burke's *Musical Landscapes* with a foreword by Menuhin. Her husband arrives in time to make a copy of the vital page. Like his wife he talks fast but, unlike her, he keeps his eyes on you to see how much is sinking in. Like his wife he makes a deeply conservative impression. A photocopier is the second thing campaigners buy. First comes the typewriter, then the photocopier. Then they raise money. And they change.

He hands me the Nature Conservancy Council's notification, headed by an impressive crown, formally declaring Winfrith Heath a site of Special Scientific Interest. Here, since I am new to the game, I have to slow the pace of things a moment, I have to remind myself that one government-sponsored body, the Nature Conservancy Council (the Council), is declaring the heath a sanctuary while another, the Central Electricity Generating Board (the Board), is intending, in an age of micro dimensions, to erect, on the same heath, at a minimum cost of some £1.2 billion, an atomic power station so vast that three bypasses or more will probably have to be completed before the materials can be carted in to build it; so vast that it will be visible from as far off as North Dorset, Bournemouth and the New Forest.

For we are not only talking of cooling towers. We have not mentioned turbine buildings two hundred and thirty foot high, access roads, car parks, canteens, sewerage and huge paved areas, none of which are normally held to be compatible with the preservation of a unique piece of Dorset's vanishing heathland celebrated for its rare animals and the undisturbed evolution of its plant life. But then I hadn't realised either, until my host told me, that nobody from the Board, so far as the Bridges know, ever consulted the people who lived on the land which the new plant would devastate. Nobody from the Board made a survey or took borings. Nobody in fact showed the smallest human or social or topographical curiosity in the place, until after the Board's intention was formally unveiled. Or if anybody did, no word of this has reached the Bridges.

'The Board gave an exhibition in the village hall but it was not sufficiently site-specific,' says David Bridges, in the factual language he is careful to employ when speaking of The Threat. 'They were simply selling nuclear power.'

His wife is a mite less guarded. 'They sent spokesmen down who'd never been here before and they addressed the community as if we were peasants. They were not popular at all.'

Dragged by accident into the public relations business, the Bridges are anxious I should appreciate the eminently respectable character of the opposition to The Threat. The 'Winfrith Heath Committee' is supported by, among other bodies, the Parish Council, the Purbeck District Council and representatives and agents of the largest local landowners. Help and money have also come from the trustees of the Weld Estate. Strategic advice has come from the Council for the Protection of Rural England (CPRE), who also had the idea of producing this book. Lulworth is the most spectacular coastal beauty spot in Dorset and the most celebrated. It lies three miles from the intended power station. The Bridges are particularly anxious I should not describe them as anti-nuclear. From the outset, the infant committee took two very shrewd decisions of principle. It would not enter the anti-nuclear lobby and make friends it might not wish to live with. It would not involve itself in suggesting alternative sites and make enemies it didn't need. And though I could not help noticing that the name of Chernobyl had found its way into at least one of the handouts, they are keeping very quiet about health risks too. The Bridges' nightmare is seven years old. Until seven years ago the Parish Council of Winfrith, like any other, was tearing itself apart with such crucial problems as where to erect a new signpost or paint a white line. Today old feuds and rivalries are put aside, and the detail of a past and peaceful life is dispatched as other business. Today they are united and mobilised and alert as never before. They have taken the shock course in strategy, and so far they have passed with flying colours.

'A councillor said to me, "Now I know how a mouse feels when a cat is playing with it",' says a brighter David Bridges, set free by the open air. We are plodding over the 'designated area' – the site of The Threat. While he talks, he interrupts his own flow to point out the glories he feels we should know about: carnivorous plants, commonly known as sundew, which use sticky liquid to catch insects; the nursery stream, rich in salmon and sea trout. This is not the parrot talk of an official spokesman, but the impassioned communication of a lifelong naturalist. He recites the species of birds that have made the heath their habitat: bittern, hen harriers, marsh harriers, nightjar, curlew and buzzard. Strewn around us are the broomstick aerials of the radiation monitors painted a discreet green. Above us, behind ranks of wind-dwarfed conifers, looms Winifrith's original nuclear research station, built in the Fifties when we knew even less about atomic energy than we do now. 'Stack it four times on itself and you get the cooling towers,' says David Bridges. But he is careful to speak kindly of the Atomic Energy Establishment staff who run it:

'We enjoy a good relationship with them. When the old people in the village were flooded out, they lent us special equipment. When the electricity failed, they cooked us hot meals in their kitchens.'

Nevertheless, he believes that the presence of the old research station explains the Board's selection of Winfrith as the site for their present project. 'They reckoned they would meet with less resistance if the Atomic Energy Establishment was here already,' he says. He knows of no other reason for the choice except that it would be handy for the National Grid. Winfrith's sparsely populated hinterland alone could not consume the extra power. The transmission costs of getting it to distant urban areas would be vast. As to the £1.2 billion – 'if they've got it to spare, let them spend it on energy conservation.' That's as far as he'll go towards suggesting an alternative.

'February 1980 was our first word of it. The Board sent the Parish Council the transcript of an announcement they proposed to make that same day. The letter arrived at 8.00 a.m.'

Here I should tell you a little more about David Bridges for I am not sure that even he understands the irony of his situation. He is a vital but careful man, dressed in careful greys, and very community-minded. He could be a teacher or a scoutmaster. For all I know he has been both, for he speaks a lot about the groups of children he has taken to the heath to show them its wonders. But his main job is that of chartered surveyor with the local authority, to which he adds the relatively humble appointment of Clerk to Winfrith Parish Council. It is sheer luck – to him, perhaps, bad luck, though I am not so sure – but for the Winfrith Heath Committee a Godsend – that the front windows of his thatched cottage look straight at the threatened heath not a hundred yards across the road. The Board's letter, therefore, which in ordinary circumstances would have struck unprepared and humble citizens too late, landed, not on the breakfast plate of an appalled postman or undertaker, but of an agile-minded, nature-loving public servant with twenty years' acquaintance with the ways of bureaucrats and businessmen.

'The letter didn't say where the conference was being held but I rang a press friend and went. It was in a quiet pub in the town, and when I got there the Board's spokesman was describing how they would use landscape architects to reduce the impact of the building. I was too shocked to do much, but I did manage to ask one question: "How do you reduce the impact of a building three hundred and sixty feet high?" They agreed it would be difficult.'

David Bridges is a different man now. He is battle-wise and he handles himself, as they say. But his experience has cut him off. The remorseless unlogic that has surrounded him for so long has entered his soul:

'How can you build in a designated rural area and keep it rural or worth designating? How can you build motorways that erode the beauties people have come to see?' Then, like many people with a mission, he worries, and apologises for getting on his hobby horse, even while he rides it a little harder. 'Only you see, I know it sounds pompous, but the integrity of Dorset is really under threat.' His experience of bureaucracy has taught him to worry about something else as well: 'And when they *do* get to the point where they would logically recognise their error, they're going to be so entrenched they won't be able to. How are they going to get out of this without losing face? They can't.'

He is talking about the pollution. The Board originally claimed that the towers would emit only steam. Now they're testing. But to get water, unless they divert it from the river Frome, they must go to the sea. If they do that, millions of gallons of sea water will be evaporated by the cooling towers every day. Either way, the clouds will dominate the countryside for miles around. Also every day – if seawater is used – tons of salt will be thrown into the atmosphere. How many depends on whether demisters are to be fitted at extra cost. The daily minimum is four tons. Where would all this salt land? If there were a wind, most likely on Bournemouth. But if there were mist, the plume wouldn't rise, and most of the salt would bounce back on to Winfrith, causing havoc to trees, cattle and farmland.

To end our day we drive to the exquisite village of Moreton to see Lawrence of Arabia's grave, which commemorates him not as a man of war, but as a Fellow of All Souls. From the cemetery we pass to the tiny church. It was destroyed by a German bomb in October 1940, and has been extraordinarily well restored. The twelve windows were etched by Laurence Whistler and paid for by funds raised by the community. Whistler's theme was Light. Moreton is one and a half miles from Winfrith.

You would not immediately suppose, as you admire these superb but disturbing photographs, that they contain the drama of a modern spy story. Alas, they do. A deal of cover-up, a deal of cowardice, layer after layer of bureaucratic secrecy, but above all the dark and unrelenting struggle between man and the dreadful institutions he creates. The peaceful vales and meadows in these photographs reek of all of them. There are Winfrith Heaths right across England, whether they are threatened by nuclear power stations, oil rigs, motorways, trunk roads or thoughtless house-building. Do not be hypnotised by the nuclear connection: the conventional weapons are quite as terrible.

And you would not immediately suppose, since the photographs contain few human figures, that a single human face looks out of them. It is the face that all of us know who by an accident of life have been drawn into conflict with backroom planning, as opposed to the sort that is arrived at by public discussion while decisions are still open. It is a face that would prefer to have no name, because to have a name is to have a personal responsibility, and it is this man's refuge to plead he has none. It is the face of the British executive thug – whether he is the instrument of a state executive or of the hideously misnomered 'private sector'. How our society has produced such people is a mystery to me. So are the forces that move them towards what is lightly called a decision. Somewhere long ago, in the mind of a man promoted, knighted and retired, perhaps, a thoroughly bad idea was born. Nourished by plausible presentation, it grew and gathered strength until it was old enough to become the Official Solution to a problem that may never have existed in the first place. The Solution became a Plan, the Plan a Paper and the Paper became an object of public dispute. At this point, God help us all. For now Authority is being challenged, whether it is ministerial or big business. And a lot of people who till now had *thought* they were Authority – as voters, as taxpayers, as rate payers, as decent, middle-of-the-road English men and women – discover that they are standing in the path of a derailed bureaucratic train got up to look like progress.

Yet this book is not a moan about past failures but a battle-cry and a survivors' handbook. The English countryside lives. It has suffered dreadful casualties but there are still splendid things to preserve. There are even some past follies that can be reversed. Real, creative planning and real, open debate can still offer improvement without devastation. Farming may even, one day, be regarded as an industrial process in its own right, as labour-intensive as a modern, automated factory. The British, unlike the Dutch or Scandinavians, have not till now been good at caring about the future. They don't believe in it and they do it wistfully, like caring for the dead. They are better at defending the present, which they do well. Fine. So rather than talk a lot of soap about our children, let's bang the table about what we want for ourselves. Sometimes that frightens politicians a lot more. Children don't vote.

But we must be prepared to frighten them. We must be ready and able, collectively, to shout 'no!' – to shout 'stop!' – to tell them emphatically that some things, whatever the supposed benefits, can never, never be done. In certain classes of British society, protest has become a dirty word. But take care, because that is what the executive thug believes when you stand in the way of his motorway, his nuclear plant, his channel tunnel, his promotion or his bank account.

You want Victorian values? You think, perhaps, that the Victorians were stoical and passive when their landscape was threatened? Then perhaps you should consider the example of those Victorians who protested against the private railway acts of the 1840s, or the canal acts before them. Those were the days when thousands of established citizens, great and small – their rights, in the great Tory tradition, determined by landed or financial interest, however modest – flooded down to London, cramming the hotels and no doubt the less respectable establishments as well, while each in turn exercised his right to petition the Commons. Perhaps you should consider the campaign of direct action, inspired by such venerable Victorian founding fathers as John Stuart Mill and John Ruskin, that saved Berkhampstead Common for us in the 1860s. Or the bitter and successful fights to save other commons, around the same period, that led to the founding of the Commons, Open Footpaths & Open Spaces Preservation Society that is alive and kicking even now. Today's protester is not a troublemaker, but the inheritor of precious and very ancient rights. What could be more appropriate than using them to preserve our heritage?

The Council for the Protection of Rural England is now sixty years old. It was extremely lively before the Second World War and, like the rest of Britain, tired after it. Today as never in its history it is standing up and being counted as the strongest force in England for the preservation of individual freedom and dignity through respect for the environment. CPRE is not the gentrified equivalent of Greenpeace. It is a quieter, older brother. While Greenpeace and like bodies, with admirable courage, seize centre stage, provoke and stir, CPRE takes upon itself the softer-footed task of educating ministers and the public through constitutional argument; of rallying public opinion in the cities and in the countryside, and monitoring the sinister back-stage manoeuvring by which the big batallions of industry and government seek to withhold crucial decisions from public scrutiny. The CPRE does not frustrate development in principle. It does not seek to restore the horse-drawn carriage or turn Britain into a rustic museum. But it demands to know why things are done and it prefers the individual to the institutions he has allowed to run amok. It questions, as no partisan body can, the supposed gains of environmental devastation. Do we really need new industrial plant in the south when the north is crying for investment? What is the point of allowing the Titans of the housing lobby to eat up more and more so-called green-field sites while the inner cities, with all the wretched social consequences we know about, fall into squalor and decay? And are its long-term benefits mere pie in the sky? CPRE asks these questions and will ask them for you. It will throw you a lifeline if disaster should enter your street, as it entered that of the Bridges and their children. It will not think you silly when you speak of the integrity of your county or your village. And it will give you the comfort of experience when you feel most threatened and afraid.

There was a time when town and country people lived in a state of mutual contempt. The town man saw his country cousin as a self-regarding simpleton whose fantasies were only made possible by the hard grind of the city. And the countrymen in return saw his urban cousin as unrooted, decadent, and careless of man and nature in his rackety pursuit of wealth. Each believed he had a right to exploit the other's element to the advantage of his own. Each was wrong.

But that distinction, if I have drawn it rightly, must be dying even as we think of it. Thanks to the motorcar, virtually the whole of lowland England is already within striking range of an urban area. Commuters, second homers, the growing flood of refugees from the bloodiness of city living, migrant labour, not to mention the large British holidaymaking public that still prefers its native countryside to other people's have in recent years kicked a hole clean through such facile prejudice. The Empire too is gone, thank Heaven. No more new horizons there. No more big spaces to turn into proxy English shires. Our foreign travel – to Greece, to Spain, to Portugal, to America – too often opens our eyes to the horrors of greedy over-development. And as our horizons close again, I believe that British people are beginning to understand that they are all the inheritors of a tiny beautiful country that can only take so much destruction before it merges with the common mass. I think we are becoming decently angry about whatever it is in our system that allows such destruction to continue, to the pleasure and advantage of none except the few who perpetrate it. History, said Voltaire, is the lie that historians agree upon. By the same token, British politics are often a tacit conspiracy to do combat about carefully selected 'issues'. Yet here, before our eyes, is an issue no modern British political party has yet espoused. Constrained by their own traditions, the old parties are just beginning to grope nervously for an environmental policy. Yet they still offer no more than lip-service. The new party is no further forward. Meanwhile, our most ancient birthright – our land – is being stolen from beneath our noses. Not by an invading army. But by devolved powers. By neglect. By loophole. By apathy and by want of a commanding central vision. By faceless men in secret conclave. But finally, I am afraid, by ourselves, who have too often failed to exercise the ancient rights and freedoms that were won for us by our noisier forebears, and still have to be fought for every day.

Very soon we are going to understand that the health of our countryside is as important to us as the air we breathe, the food we eat, the water we drink, the medicines we take, the doctors we visit and the politicians we vote for. The environment, or whatever word we use, will then move from the political fringe to the political mainstream. With CPRE and its fellows pulling, and the concerned public pushing, it is happening now. At that stage, our elected representatives will no longer be able to shrug it aside as the province of dreamers and crazies. They will have to shift to where the sane public stands, or take their own places at the fringe.

Country road near Warmington (Photo : Graeme Harris)

COUNTY DURHAM · *The Derwent Valley*

Heather Angel IS AN INTERNATIONALLY RECOGNISED WILDLIFE PHOTOGRAPHER AND ONE OF THE MOST EMINENT OF HER GENERATION · SHE IS A PAST PRESIDENT OF THE ROYAL PHOTOGRAPHIC SOCIETY AND AN HONORARY DOCTOR OF SCIENCE AT BATH UNIVERSITY

Once, it is said, a red squirrel could pass from one end of England to the other, from tree to tree in an unbroken medieval forest. Today the creature could still make uninterrupted progress through a replica of that ancient tree mantle, the abundantly wooded valley of the Derwent in Northumberland.

The trees, sessile oak, ash and birch, are the glory of the Derwent Valley. They have dominated it since at least 1600. Successive generations have nurtured and protected these trees: the 300-year-old Chopwell Wood, despite its name, is as vigorous today as it ever was. Wherever the magnificent stands were cleared for timber, they were always replaced; or where they were coppiced for charcoal-burning, allowed to regenerate.

The greatest harvest of timber was taken during the reign of George III, when trees from the valley were cut to build vessels to counter an invasion from France. But the landowners of the day, the Strathmores and the Bowes, left a magnificent legacy – saplings planted to replace the lost trees have now grown to their full and splendid maturity.

Such richness in trees in a river valley is rare in England, more so in the industrial north-east where man has turned the valley bottoms of such rivers as the Tees and Tyne into dreary, wasted, deforested places. The Derwent is wooded throughout its length, from its source 1,700 feet up at Allenheads in Northumberland to the river Tyne thirty-five miles away.

The semi-natural woodland of the Derwent is more than a visual thrill; it is a rich habitat for wildlife. A single oak-tree may harbour as many as 280 insect species in its life, and overspread a distinct community of woodland plants such as dog's mercury and wood anemone. In such isolated pockets of woodland as this in the north of England the native red squirrel is found, betraying its presence with a discarded hazelnut shell.

The Derwent Valley, south-east of Newcastle upon Tyne, has been exploited, especially in its lower reaches, by coal-miners and steel-makers; but these were small-scale enterprises at works in the ownership of great industrialists who lived there, men like the Bowes at Gibside Hall in its setting of finely wooded ravines and slopes, with its grandiose 140-feet-high statue to British liberty. Living in the valley, these proprietors took care not to deface it.

Even the coming of the North-Eastern Railway Company's eleven-mile branch line spared this delicate valley. It was a place of production and output for the departing trains, carrying coal from the lower valley and some of the first good-quality steel in Britain.

But for those trains coming in it was a destination of ease and spiritual renewal. On the line's opening in 1867 the *Newcastle Daily Journal* advised its readers that 'the scenery opened out by this branch is of a very beautiful description'. For a shilling Tyneside trippers could enjoy a day out to see the parkland of Gibside and the remains of the thirteenth-century manor at Old Hollinside, one of the few fortified manor-houses from the Middle Ages to survive in the north-east.

The line, closed now, has become the Derwent Walk, a traffic-free avenue of stupendous vantage-points down the entire valley. Hamsterley Viaduct, one of four in the valley, provides some of the finest views over trees in the county. Below the off-white brickwork of the viaduct is spread the muddle of trees for many purposes: cosmetic, in the carefully arranged parkland in the grounds of Hamsterley Hall; productive, in the ancient stands of Chopwell Wood; functional, as wind-breaks and bank stabilisers along the riverside. Close to this point, at the spa at Shotley Bridge, swordmakers from Solingen in Germany, who had fled religious persecution, harnessed the swift-flowing river, cut the oaks for charcoal and smelted local ore.

The Roman road from York to Edinburgh, Dere Street, crossed the Derwent Valley higher up, at Ebchester, guarding the place with the square, four-acre fort of Vindomora. Later, stones from the fort were used to build houses in the village. There is a Roman altar built into the Norman church tower. Archaeologists have detected from the air the lines of a network of Roman roads radiating from Ebchester and the tantalising outline of a previously unknown Roman fort to the north-west.

Throughout the Derwent Valley there is a prime-quality coal close to the surface. The result : increasing pressure from British Coal and others to extract it by open-cast mining methods. CPRE has campaigned continuously against this – successfully so far. Open-cast mining is environmentally very damaging and full land restoration is not possible.

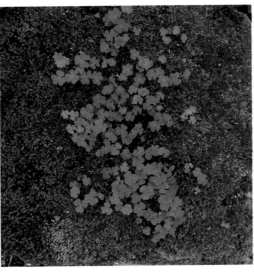

TOP *Coatgate Burn flowing through fern-covered rocks and hazel foliage*
ABOVE *Wood sorrel on a moss-covered stump, photographed in the Derwent Valley*
LEFT *Summer view of wild meadow flowers from Wittonstall in the Derwent Valley*

TOP *Cotton grass in fruit at Waldridge Fen – the last of the great moors in lowland Durham*
ABOVE *Meadow flowers growing against a wall with rose-bay willow-herb behind*
RIGHT *The river Derwent near Allenford, Tyne and Wear*

North Devon

DURING THE PAST FIFTEEN YEARS *Clive Arrowsmith* HAS WORKED

FOR ALL THE WORLD'S MAJOR MAGAZINES AND HAS PHOTOGRAPHED

MANY OF THE WORLD'S MOST FAMOUS PERSONALITIES · LANDSCAPES ARE

A NEW DEPARTURE FOR HIM AND THE QUALITY OF HIS WORK IS

A REFLECTION OF HIS SKILL, SENSITIVITY AND CRAFTSMANSHIP

Close to Ash Mill in North Devon, a gentle green place caressed by low hills which fold neatly behind one another into the distance, the Atlantic salmon has for years without number returned to its spawning-ground in the Crooked Oak river. In another of this valley's steady routines red deer troop off the cold moors to their winter feeding-grounds here.

It is a fresh, unpolluted country, of sensible, unextravagant farming. In one of its secret corners, the miniature side-shoot valley of the Sturcombe stream, moss and lichen grow as indicators of crystal-clear air on the trunks of the stunted oak, birch and hazel which fringe it. The lesser celandine, with its glossy yellow flowers, and the primrose press through the crunching carpet of fallen leaves in the spring.

On Hare's Down at the top of the valley of the Crooked Oak, between South Molton and Tiverton, nature is trapped in a time warp. Here scientists may study plant communities which have been anchored to their soil for the past 1,000 years or more. While man has made some modest changes to the surrounding countryside, Hare's Down and the adjoining Knowstone Moor have survived undefiled, a rare example of nature's uninterrupted work over the centuries. In the heathland plants found here may be locked secrets of our natural environment, to be revealed through scientific techniques yet to be devised.

Hare's Down and Knowstone Moors are an internationally important mosaic of wet and dry heathland vegetation on a complex undulating landscape. They are part of the Culm

Measures, one of the largest and most ecologically diverse remnants left in Britain of a type of ancient heathland now confined to the British Isles, Brittany and Normandy.

The heath overlies a mixture of sandstones, stones and slates which form pockets of dissimilar soils, each supporting their associated specialised plants. This was a habitat once widely distributed in England; but these heaths have been reclaimed over the centuries leaving only a few scattered islands of heathland, surrounded by improved land.

This habitat is now confined mainly to the south-west, nurtured by the soothing moist oceanic climate and the relative mildness of its winters. Hare's Down and Knowstone are common land and have been spared cultivation. Men have maintained them with a careful hand, cutting, burning and grazing in proper season.

A walk of only a few yards will reveal fresh and distinctive micro habitats, with different species responding to subtle variations in altitude, soil formation, slope and aspect. Some specialised plants grow only in the acid soil in the harsh environment on the crown of the moor – purple moor grass, bell-heather, western gorse, deer grass and sphagnum moss.

The sentinels of the heathland nest and feed here – nightjar, stonechat, whinchat, redstart and tree pipit. The open land draws in the hunting birds, the tawny owl, buzzard, sparrow-hawk, out of their breeding places in the wooded fringe. Herds of a dozen or more red deer patrol Hare's Down. In summer the hinds secrete their calves in the safe bracken.

The prize among twenty-eight species of butterfly found on the moors is the marsh fritillary, now scarce throughout Britain. It feeds uniquely on the devil's bit scabious which is common on the moors. It is extremely vulnerable, living in small colonies, each with a kingdom no bigger than a small field.

The moors are areas of the highest nature calibre. They are among the 4,800 or so small pockets of land, ranging from a few to thousands of acres, designated Sites of Special Scientific Interest by the Government's nature agency, the Nature Conservancy Council, for their biological and geological importance. Sites of Special Scientific Interest include the best examples in Britain of particular habitats, such as woodlands, heathlands or meadows, and the habitats of rare and endangered species or important concentrations of animals or plants. Furthermore, the moors are among just 700 areas included in the NCC's *Nature Conservation Review* as prime examples of wild habitat to be preserved at all costs.

The Department of Transport has approved the building of the North Devon Link Road between South Molton and Tiverton down the valley of the Crooked Oak and bisecting the heath of Hare's Down. The new road will devastate some of the West Country's most beautiful landscape and diminish the value of an internationally important wildlife site.

PAGES 22 TO 25 *Land between Taunton and Moretonhampstead where the North Devon Link Road will cut a swaithe through some of Devon's most beautiful countryside*

DEVON · *The Dart Estuary*

PROBABLY ENGLAND'S BEST KNOWN PHOTOGRAPHER,

David Bailey IS PASSIONATELY COMMITTED TO THE

CONSERVATION OF THE COUNTRYSIDE · HE HAS BEEN INTERESTED IN

LANDSCAPE PHOTOGRAPHY FOR MANY YEARS AND IS

DEEPLY CONCERNED ABOUT THE THREAT TO THE RIVER DART

There are only a few places in England where the tide flows as delicately and gracefully, deep into unspoilt England, as in the valley of the Dart. At first it comes with force and fury, around Blackstone Point and the Mew Stone. By One Gun Point and Half Tide Rock its vigour is diminishing. By the time it passes Kingswear and Dartmouth, tucked within the estuary's calming mouth, it bears its surroundings little malice.

On and on it flows, diverting up utterly remote backwaters, like Old Mill Creek, silent sites of former shipyards, now the haunt of herons and the occasional seal. Up it flows, past Lower Noss Point, the Anchor Stone and Parson's Mud, to regions totally untouched by development. Below Dittisham the steep wooded slopes press down from the neatly parcelled fields over 500 feet up, to resemble a fiord.

Famous Elizabethan seafarers, the Gilbert brothers, John, Humphrey and Adrian, lived above these waters and understood their depths before they ventured out into the Atlantic. Their half-brother Sir Walter Raleigh would have tested the river on his visits. Another illustrious Elizabethan explorer, John Davis, was born in the valley. Davis looked for the North-west Passage and found the Davis Strait off west Greenland. Later the crime thriller writer Agatha Christie lived in a house above the valley.

The enclosing land releases its squeeze on the tide where it breaks out into the wide, open curve of Flat Owers. The river creeps across silt-flats of good Devon earth washed down from

---

the steep hills over the years. Boats recline at anchor on these mud-flats, close to old oyster-farms and a mussel bed. The tide slips gently by Blackness Rock, past Pighole Point and over the Middle Back mud-flats below Whitestone Farm where dunlin, ringed plover, curlew and godwits probe the protein-rich mud before the advancing waters.

On it flows, past the hillside village of Ashprington, to which the Domesday Book attributes two fisheries on the river, probably salmon. The Dart makes two bends of a slithering snake; above them the tide is into the final straight, untroubled reaches, abundant in fish where migrating osprey find a temporary haven in the autumn.

The limit of the rising tide's influence is eleven miles from the open sea, on the straight thrust into Totnes. The town is still served by sea-going vessels. Once its maritime trade made it the fifteenth richest town in England. It still contains more listed buildings per head of population than any other town in England.

The Dart, the finest of Devon's ten estuaries, is a ria or deep-sided drowned valley, cut by melt-waters during the Ice Age, then flooded as water-levels rose when the ice finally melted. Submerged and raised ledges and cliffs are the evidence of how the water-level has risen and fallen over the millennia. The estuary forms part of the South Devon Area of Outstanding Natural Beauty, designated in 1960 in recognition of the fine river landscape and its wider setting of tumbling hills.

The farming on the hills above the river is benign and undemanding, much given to sheep, sparing the land the heavy wear on the lowland cereal fields elsewhere in England. Men have played their part in contributing to the estuary's beauty, cloaking the hillsides with woodland over the past two centuries. There is Gallant's Bower, a wooded knoll above the estuary at Dartmouth. Oyers Hill and Hoodown are deciduous woods of oak, beech and sweet chestnut. Near the harbour entrance is a formidable stand of Monterey pines, natives of California, as much at home as these trees will ever be in England on this south-facing site.

The link with the original wooded mantle is to be found in Long Wood, owned by the National Trust, an ancient oak-wood, more than 300 years old. Once it was coppiced and its bark used in the tanning of leather and to make charcoal for smelting metals. It is a Site of Special Scientific Interest and one of the best-surviving examples of the oak-wood of the lower Dart Valley.

To the sailor the estuary has always been a place of hope and salvation, the best refuge from the prevailing westerly winds between Plymouth and Portland Bill. It is a natural harbour, with no sand-bar: it promises deep water at any state of the tide. The surrounding hills ensure the calm.

Dartmouth's prosperity as a port dates from the twelfth century, when it grew to meet the needs of military and commercial shipping. The harbour entrance is guarded by the two castles of Dartmouth and Kingswear, built in the fourteenth century to keep the French out during the Hundred Years War. John Hawley, wine merchant, mayor and bold seaman, and believed to be the inspiration for Chaucer's Shipman in *The Canterbury Tales*, lived in the town.

The port was used in the twelfth century as a point of assembly and departure for 164 vessels leaving for the Second and Third Crusades. Trade was stimulated by the acquisition of south-west France by Henry II's marriage in 1152. The early export of cloth from Totnes and the import of wine from Spain and France made it the fourth wealthiest town in Devon. Prosperity was sustained over the centuries through the trade in slate, tin, cloth, hides and coal. In 1180 Totnes exported down the Dart 800,000 slates for the building of Winchester Castle and a further 100,000 for Porchester. By the late sixteenth and early seventeenth centuries local sailors carried out a triangular trade, taking cod from Newfoundland to the Mediterranean and carrying wine back home.

Within their geographical constraints the port and river have adapted to changing circumstances. When commercial trade fell off with the introduction of the bigger ships it could not accommodate, the port turned to the coal-bunkering trade, serving the passing steamboats. For a time there was a passenger and mail service to South Africa and Australia. Today there is only the occasional link with the past when, about twenty times a year, a bright red Baltic timber ship steals up to Totnes on the high tide, its practised master negotiating the tortuous twists in the river with inches to spare.

There are now plans to build a large deep-water port at Noss Point, close to Long Wood in the river Dart estuary. The construction of the port and its associated buildings would damage a delicate environment and popular recreation area. The influx of large ships would intrude into the peace of the valley, and the transport of cargoes would create serious traffic problems on narrow roads leading to the river through beautiful countryside.

PAGES 29 TO 33 *Commercial development of the Dart estuary will have a serious impact on the whole area. David Bailey's pictures show both the open countryside to the east of the estuary as well as the woods and river banks close to the proposed site*

LINCOLNSHIRE · *Fulbeck*

BASED IN DERBY, *John Blakemore*

LECTURES IN ART AT THE DERBY LONSDALE COLLEGE · HIS LANDSCAPES

HAVE BEEN EXHIBITED EXTENSIVELY BOTH IN ONE-MAN

AND GROUP EXHIBITIONS. THE ISSUE OF THE DUMPING OF NUCLEAR WASTE IS

PARTICULARLY NEAR TO HIS HEART AND HE HAS BEEN CLOSELY

ASSOCIATED WITH THE CAMPAIGN TO PROTECT FULBECK

It is not wise to prejudge the English landscape. Lincolnshire, a county which the innocent may assume to be flat, can offer some of the most stimulating views in lowland Britain. There is a long, thin belt of high ground pointing north from Grantham to Lincoln. The Romans first took control of it, appropriately driving a highway along it, the arrow-straight Ermine Street, or High Dyke, north to Lincoln, from Anchester. But the top is exposed and open to the bitter north-east winds. Nobody chose to live there. Geography offered a compromise. The land switchbacks away from the crown of the ridge to the west onto a second, lower shelf of raised ground. On this a string of communities was built, the cliff villages of Fulbeck, Caythorpe, Carlton Scroop, Leadenham and Hough-on-the-Hill.

From any of these villages there is a long prospect stretching away over a neat patchwork of farmland. In the grey-blue northern distance is the massive landmark of Lincoln Cathedral. It stands sideways to the observer in the south and almost a tenth of a mile long, built on a hill which rises, striking and quite alone, out of the limestone on which the city is built. The view runs unbroken down to the west over the Trent Valley, past the low villages of Stragglethorpe, Brant Broughton, Brandon, Stubton and Claypole, and south-west across the thin restless line of the Great North Road to Belvoir thirteen miles away. In its season, when the crops are low, the famous Belvoir hunt sweeps across the Trent plain, as far as the cliff villages. A perilous activity this – Sir Watkin Winn lies at Fulbeck Church, killed while hunting in 1825.

This is a well-farmed country, rich and obliging. The Fane family at Fulbeck Manor has worked their 2,700-acre estate for 350 years. Today the Fanes are repaying the generosity of the fields by coaxing back some of the wildlife which has been swept off the English landscape by modern farming. Local road verges are allowed to grow into rambling summer plenty and are not cut before 1 July to allow cowslips and other spring-germinating wild flowers to set their seed. This brings on a flush of wild scabious and knapweed which encourages butterflies in late August and September.

Where hedges run from north to south, and there is no problem of shade to growing crops, they are allowed to grow full and high, as nesting habitat and song perches for birds. Elsewhere new trees grow from selected untrimmed saplings in the hedges. In the first year a single green stem rises above the cut hedge; within five it has the makings of a substantial tree, its roots already well-established in the hedge.

In some corners of the estate they are putting the countryside back together again. Seven acres, wasted for over forty years since the Royal Air Force placed their wartime huts on this site, have been replanted with oak-trees, with Scots pine acting as a nurse crop to deflect the keen Lincolnshire winds. The old abandoned railway line which once linked these villages is reverting to nature. Up on the ridge is Big Wood, its old trees safe from any quick-profit clearance: a thick carpet of aconites pushes up in the early spring. This rural renovation work has won the Fane estate the Lincolnshire Agricultural Society's Farm Conservation Award. The lord of the manor, Julian Fane, used the money to create two ponds which are already busy with invading wildlife.

The collection of villages, close enough to enjoy a loose identity, are distant enough from towns to be entirely rural. Caythorpe and Fulbeck, at their centre, are in the middle of a triangle formed by Newark to the west, Sleaford to the east, Lincoln to the north and Grantham to the south.

Many of the enduring features of village life are here. There is a valiant cricket team at Fulbeck which fought through to the later rounds of a national competition recently. There is at Stragglethorpe a blacksmith who works behind bright blue doors. His is not a contrived throw-back to a more traditional village life, but a flourishing, real business.

Caythorpe is the key village with a population of 1,500. Villagers care deeply about their community life and their facilities, so these communities share riches indeed. Caythorpe people have the choice of three pubs, a fish and chip shop, a village hall, a primary school and four doctors. It receives a travelling bank and a mobile library. It has an architecturally eccentric church: from a distance St Vincent's swollen spire looks like a Jules Verne space rocket. Inside it has an unusual feature, a fourteenth-century nave arcade.

Fulbeck, smaller, with a population of 500, is an officially designated conservation area, prettily built in the local creamy-yellow brick. It has the well-preserved church of St Nicholas, restored when it was needed, containing Saxon features, a peal of six bells and many monuments to the Fane family.

At Leadenham, where the main road from Newark to Sleaford struggles up on to the limestone plateau, there are two ample Georgian inns to cater for the crossroads traffic.

These villages have collided with history. A rector at Fulbeck Church, Master John Dyghton, appointed by Henry VII, is said to have murdered the two princes in the Tower. In 1944 the airfields on the Trent plain became an important point of departure for that heroic lost cause, the raid on Arnhem. Men from the First Airborne Signals were billeted in Fulbeck. Every year the veterans return, a brave, diminishing company.

Just above one of those old wartime bases, Fulbeck Airfield, another long journey begins. The Sand Beck flows off the high ground at Hough-on-the-Hill, cuts through the airfield, then passes into the river Brand, which flows on into the Witham which twists and curves down through rich vegetable-growing Lincolnshire, eventually to reach Boston and The Wash.

The disused Fulbeck Airfield, close to Stragglethorpe in the valley below the cliff villages, is one of the new – and highly controversial – research sites for a dump for low-level nuclear waste. It is one of four such sites in England currently under investigation by the nuclear industry, all of which have aroused passionate opposition. Apart from the unforseeable risks of contamination, particularly into the Sand Beck which passes through the airfield, the entire community of surrounding villages would be blighted for centuries to come by the creation of such a dump. A rural serenity would be replaced with deep doubt and unease.

PAGES 37 TO 39 *The peaceful East Anglian countryside around Fulbeck shows the close relationship between agriculture and conservation. The landscape has obviously been cherished and cared for by the local community*

ESSEX · *Tillingham Hall*

BORN IN SCOTLAND, *Peter Cattrell* NOW LECTURES ON

PHOTOGRAPHY AT ST MARTIN'S COLLEGE OF ART IN LONDON · HE HAS HELD SEVERAL

EXHIBITIONS OF URBAN AND RURAL LANDSCAPES AND IS A

PARTICULARLY SKILFUL EXPONENT OF 'FINE PRINT TECHNIQUE'

Tillingham Hall is a remote Essex farm on the most westerly nudge of the East Anglian Fens. Three miles further on, London shudders to a well-defined halt. There is no wandering suburbia: from this boundary the English countryside makes a clean and determined escape from the capital's grip, like a sprinter off his blocks.

Tillingham is a place of wide horizons and unimpeded winds. In winter there is a raw starkness over the fields and drainage dykes, too hard-edged to inspire the landscape-artist but a place of great solace for the city-bound. In summer it offers a flourishing pastoral prospect. Place a blindfolded walker on the footpaths which wind along the low hedges and he need never know that this place stands so close to one of the most populous cities on Earth. Round about it are the names which could have been carved out of any rural map: Little Malgraves, Mar Dyke, Blankets, Orsett Fen, Old England.

The village of Bulphan is on the southern edge of Tillingham Hall Farm, about six miles north of Tilbury on the river Thames. There is the profound atmosphere of escape here. Bulphan is a bolt-hole, untouched by the vast metropolitan hubbub close to the west. It is not on the road to, or from, anywhere really significant. A trunk-road skirts it to the east and few outsiders ever trouble it. It is a village of no immediately conspicuous merit, but like many equally modest English communities it has a notable history, traced back to the Domesday Survey. And as in many English villages there is an independence casually displayed to the outside world, but defended with a great passion by those who live there.

It is no accident that the eastern march of the metropolis did not swallow up the farm and the village long ago. Tillingham Hall is in a prime tract of Green Belt. No single piece of planning policy has done more to protect the English countryside than the Green Belt. Its inspiration lies deep in history. Queen Elizabeth I expressed the imperious wish to check 'the city of great multitudes'. Christopher Wren had visions of a green girdle surrounding the London that was to arise from the ashes of the Great Fire of London. In Queen Victoria's reign the City of London Corporation raised duty on coal and wine sales to buy common land in the recreational areas outside the capital, such as Epping Forest and Burnham Beeches.

The Green Belt was conceived as a policy priority in the 1930s and the leader of the old London County Council, Herbert Morrison, proposed a reservoir of land around the capital. It was first officially promoted by housing minister, Duncan Sandys, in a 1955 circular: 'For the well-being of our people and for the preservation of our countryside, we have a clear duty to prevent the unrestricted sprawl of the great cities.'

The purpose of the Green Belt is to check the advance of built-up areas, to prevent neighbouring towns running together, and to safeguard the countryside from encroachment. To the city-dweller it ensures that there are areas of open land within easy reach. To developers it represents an exclusion zone upon which they cannot transgress. Building is not allowed in the Green Belt except in special circumstances, and villages may not be extended.

Over the past eight years London's Green Belt has been redefined and reduced in area by about fifteen per cent, although this protective green girdle is still three times bigger than London itself. In other parts of England it protects the rural skirts of Manchester, Birmingham, Sheffield, Oxford, Cambridge, York and Bristol.

The Green Belt is not concerned with the quality of the landscape it preserves; it is a positive statement that the country around built-up areas, whatever its scenic or historical merit, should remain exactly as it is. As the London Green Belt Council, a body of conservationists, defines it: 'The purpose of Green Belts is to be there.' Those living in it, or several miles away in towns and cities, defend it with equal fervour.

Without the Green Belt London would by now have marched unchecked and all-consuming to the Essex coast, absorbing whatever settlement lay in its path and filling in the green spaces, to become a many-legged spider of development.

A consortium of nine of Britain's largest building companies has applied for permission to build a new town of 5,000 houses on 760 acres of open farmland at Tillingham Hall. If approved by the Government, it could be the first of a bracelet of up to fifteen new commuter towns circling London and would devastate the principle of the Green Belt throughout England, as CPRE argued, when leading objectors at the public inquiry into the scheme in 1986.

Corner of a quiet cornfield in the late summer at Tillingham Hall, Essex

The parish church at Bulphan, close to Tillingham Hall, Essex

Scarecrow in deep midwinter at Tillingham Hall, Essex

Hard frost in the corner of a field at Tillingham Hall, Essex

LANCASHIRE · *Eldon Hill*

A WELL ESTABLISHED AND HIGHLY ORIGINAL LANDSCAPE PHOTOGRAPHER BASED IN MANCHESTER, **John Davies** *IS PARTICULARLY WELL KNOWN FOR HIS PHOTOGRAPHIC ESSAYS ON THE PEAK DISTRICT NATIONAL PARK*

Midway between Sheffield and Manchester there is a buffer of wilderness, softened by flat, fair valleys. This is the spine of England, the base of the Pennines.

Just north of Eldon Hill the geological ingredients which form this pioneer national park change abruptly. A series of fine rounded hills, among them Eldon Hill, are the northernmost bastions of the great limestone plateau stretching many miles to the south. They are bounded to the north by a wide shallow valley. Its opposite side is defined by another series of equally strong prominent landmarks in gritstone and shale, two of the most celebrated of which are Rushup Edge and Mam Tor.

The opposition of these two landscapes, gritstone to the north and limestone to the south, confronting each other across an open valley, is one of the most outstanding features of the Peak District. In its scale this conspicuous change in geological gear is unique in this national park. The areas of gritstone are the magnificent, dour heights of the Peak District, known as the Dark Peak, a horseshoe of millstone grit which breaks out in solemn edges, or ridges, turned inwards. It encloses a second Peak District in the centre and south, the White Peak, consisting of pearly white limestone. This is the oldest of the Peak District rocks, created from the minute fossilised remains of creatures which lived in the shallow tropical sea which covered the centre of England in prehistoric times.

The White Peak is a soft, delicate compact country of pretty villages, broad green pastures behind grey limestone walls, with spectacular deep-sided dales, clefts and dingles. The brooding wide moors of the Dark Peak, managed for red grouse, are criss-crossed by drystone walls and streams and dotted with tors, ending abruptly at the Peakland edges, walls of gritstone rock, and drained by rocky valleys or cloughs.

The Peak District represents the beginning, or the end, of Highland Britain depending on whether the traveller approaches it from the south or the north. Daniel Defoe described the Peak in 1724–6 as 'the most desolate, wild and abandoned country in all England'. The twenty million annual visitors might question his description; the Peak is the most popular of Britain's ten national parks. It was the first park to be designated, in 1951, because of its size (524 square miles) and central position, hemmed in by South and West Yorkshire, Derbyshire and Greater Manchester, the Potteries and the West Midlands. Within fifty miles of its heart lives half the population of England.

The Hobhouse Committee, whose deliberations on how to honour the grandest and most remote of our upland wildernesses led to the creation of the parks under the 1949 National Parks and Access to the Countryside Act, described it thus: 'Beyond its intrinsic qualities, the Peak District has a unique value as a national park surrounded on all sides by towns and cities. There is no other area that has evoked more strenuous public effort to safeguard its beauty. Its very proximity to the industrial towns renders it as vulnerable as it is valuable.'

Eldon Hill, one of the highest points on the Peak District limestone, is a singular feature in this area of elevated splendour. The land around it is an area of great geological interest and natural beauty, countryside which is exceptionally distinguished even in such a well-favoured national park as this.

In 1943 the National Trust bought 463 acres of Mam Tor and the Winnats on the other side of the valley from Eldon Hill. Mam Tor is also known as Shivering Mountain. It is fraying, visibly and very dramatically, as bands of gritstone lying on softer shale are undermined by rain and frosts. The Tor is crowned by an ancient British fortified camp, built about the fifth century BC, which dominates the south-facing cliff. The Mam Tor Ridge is one of the finest viewpoints in the British Isles. The benign hand of the National Trust is in evidence in the maintenance of the farming structures and the carefully designed picnic site under the Tor.

Close to it is the Winnats Pass, a deep and spectacular dry gorge. Winnats (wind gates) is thought to have been a cave system which collapsed. It was the scene of some of the mass demonstrations to gain public access to open uplands earlier this century. Once the old turnpike road to Whaleybridge struggled up its hostile gradients, leading to Castleton and Peveril Castle, built by William Peveril, the illegitimate son of William the Conqueror.

This land is famous for its limestone swallets, or sink holes, where streams flowing off Rushup Edge sink underground. Some of the finest in the park lie along the valley between Eldon Hill and Rushup Edge – Gautries Hole, Perryfoot Cave, Jack Pot and Giant's Hole.

Early travellers were transfixed by the gaping depths of Eldon Hole. In *The Wonders of the Paeke* in 1683 Charles Cotton wrote 'This yawning mouth ... a gulf wide, steep, black and a dreadful one, which few that come to see it dare come near, and the most daring still approach with fear'. In the reign of Queen Elizabeth I the Earl of Leicester ordered a man to be lowered by ropes into the fearsome abyss. By the time he was raised he had gone mad. He died shortly afterwards.

Four miles to the north is Kinder Scout. Kinder, the highest point in the park at 2,088 feet, is a place of reverence in the ramblers' annals, and the most heavily visited open country in the park. It is divided by peat channels or groughs and forms the daunting, boggy start of the Pennine Way which leads eventually to Scotland. Other notable land-forms are the blind dry valleys of Perry Dale, Conies Dale and Cave Dale. Once these smoothed valleys carried surface rivers flowing over frozen ground during the last Ice Age.

ABOVE *Shafts of sunlight on Eldon Hill show the dreadful scarring of the landscape*
OPPOSITE *Close-up of the mine workings taken from the B6061 road at Eldon Hill*
OVERLEAF *Eldon Hill quarry photographed from Rushup Edge*

From ancient times men have won lime and lead from the Peaks, but these old workings were on a small scale and the landscape suffered little injury. Today the power of modern machinery gashes out the high-grade limestone which lies, easily released, under the thin soil.

Eldon Hill quarry, which opened in 1937 only three miles from Mam Tor, has been described as a disastrous incident in an otherwise unspoilt scene, as one of the most conspicuous eyesores in this or any national park – indeed, new quarrying is not normally allowed in national parks at all. The Government permitted limestone working at the quarry to continue when the owners made an application in 1952 to extend operations, on condition that they ended in 1997. An application has now been made by the owners for a further nine-acre extension to the quarry, which would continue its life indefinitely. If permission is granted, any possibility of repairing the massive scar on the landscape at Eldon Hill will recede into the remote future.

SUFFOLK · *The Orwell Estuary*

Terence Donovan IS ONE OF BRITAIN'S GREATEST AND

BEST KNOWN PORTRAIT AND FASHION PHOTOGRAPHERS· HIS WORK HAS BEEN

FEATURED IN ALL THE MAJOR INTERNATIONAL MAGAZINES AND

HE HAS RECENTLY DIVERSIFIED INTO FILM DIRECTION· DONOVAN HAS A

PARTICULARLY STRONG ASSOCIATION WITH THE EAST ANGLIAN COUNTRYSIDE

Even on those short winter days of pinching cold the river Orwell is a jostling, clammering, happy place for birds. They have converged from vast voyages from the far north, redshank, shelduck, dunlin, golden plover, ringed plover and turnstones from their summer territories in Greenland, Iceland and Russia, to this precious haven. The extensive mud-flats and salt-marshes of the Orwell are internationally renowned as wintering-grounds for migrating birds. A temporary population of up to 20,000 wildfowl and waders crowd on to this, one of the last remaining unspoilt estuaries in south-east England.

This is a finely balanced ecological system, one of the most natural habitats and the least affected by man left in Britain. Deep and pitted with creeks, this estuary has remained unspoilt because men found it more convenient to go elsewhere. It has remained remote and inaccessible, as travellers pressed inland to find crossings to the Orwell and the other Suffolk rivers, the Blyth, Alde, Butley and Deben.

The Orwell is remarkable among estuaries. It has steeper banks and more stretches of cliff than others, along with the more usual features of shallow water, mud-flats and marshes, which give the estuary a unique scenic quality. The river begins life as the Gipping, high up in Suffolk. It slides through solid trading towns, such as Stowmarket and Needham Market, before changing both name and character as it passes through Ipswich, where it becomes the wide tidal Orwell. The town has ancient rights over it, granted by Henry VIII.

It is one of John Constable's rivers. The artist would have walked and ridden its banks; his *View on the Orwell, at Ipswich* is in the Victoria and Albert Museum. Thomas Gainsborough painted from the hills above it: ideas in sketches he made at Hog Highland, downriver from Ipswich, were incorporated in such paintings as the *Market Cart*. On this bank is Broke Hall. It was a Broke who commanded the *Shannon* in the battle with the Chesapeake in Boston Bay in 1813. On the other side, across from Butterman's Bay, the deepest part of the river, is Pin Mill where many of the famous Thames barges were built. This has always been a flourishing river. Before the building of the railways the coal trade between Newcastle and London was monopolised by heavy Ipswich vessels called Ipswich cats which stood high and proud.

The Orwell is a river which guards its secrets, concealing its progress behind twists and curves. Developers have spared its banks: there is an unspoilt natural landscape along the full length of the estuary. There is no industrial blemish from the Orwell Bridge at Ipswich, one of the largest container ports in the country, along the seven and a half miles to beyond Fagbury Cliff, before it flows into Harwich harbour at its mouth. There are closely wooded cliffs along miles of bank, alternating with rolling fields and areas of historic parkland. Changing viewpoints reveal country houses, farmhouses and outbuildings and small villages.

The Orwell estuary merits protection under two international conventions. One is the European Commission's Directive on Bird Conservation. It is also proposed for designation under the Ramsar Convention on Wetlands, under which the Government undertakes to conserve certain vital sites, as a Site of International Importance.

The estuary's large expanses of mud, exposed at low tide at places such as Fagbury Flats, are irreplaceable feeding-grounds for waders, highly mobile birds, breeding in distant Arctic regions. The Orwell is a vital link in an international food-chain. They pass the autumn in safe moulting areas on the Dutch or German coast before wintering in such areas as these, where food, small mud-dwelling animals, can be obtained quickly in cold weather.

Nationally important numbers of five wader species visit the estuary – redshank, dunlin, turnstone, grey plover and ringed plover, and three wildfowl species, Brent goose, shelduck and pintail, as well as considerable numbers of curlew, knot and oyster-catcher. Fagbury Flats alone holds up to half of the estuary's grey plover, ringed plover and dunlin.

The Felixstowe Dock and Railway Company plans to expand its container port upstream along the banks of the river Orwell, on a 130-acre site in Trimley Marshes. The scheme has been challenged in Parliament by CPRE's branch, the Suffolk Preservation Society, and other conservation bodies. It would cause a major intrusion over ten square miles of unspoilt estuary valued for recreation, and would damage not only an outstanding landscape, but also internationally important bird feeding grounds.

OVERLEAF *Misty morning view across the fens to the estuary of the river Orwell*

The Kent Downs

Fay Godwin IS PROBABLY BRITAIN'S BEST KNOWN

LANDSCAPE PHOTOGRAPHER · SHE HAS AN INTIMATE KNOWLEDGE

OF THE KENT COUNTRYSIDE AND SHE IS PASSIONATELY

OPPOSED TO THE CHANNEL TUNNEL · SHE HAS PUBLISHED

SEVERAL BOOKS ON THE ENGLISH LANDSCAPE

The only conspicuous features of England visible from a foreign land are the white cliffs of south-east Kent. These landmarks have presented a defiant chin to the invader in wartime, and acted as a trigger of great emotion in returning patriots as long as this short neck of water has been crossed from mainland Europe.

But the chalk cliffs are more than a national symbol; they are an international rarity. Within the whole of the north-east Atlantic the prominent spectacle of the high white cliff is found elsewhere only at Cap Blanc Nez across the Channel in France, in Normandy and on the Baltic coastline. Many of the surviving white cliffs, with their associated communities of specialised plants and animals, are found in England – in Kent, Sussex, part of the Isle of Wight, Dorset and at Flamborough Head in Yorkshire.

Abbot's Cliff and Shakespeare Cliff are the best examples of chalk cliff in south-east England. They mark the ends of an enormous horseshoe of chalk, which extends westwards from the few miles of cliffs around Dover and Folkestone, across Surrey and into Hampshire where it merges with the South Downs, turning back to the east to confront the sea at Beachy Head, near Eastbourne in Sussex.

Shakespeare Cliff is a stretch of evolving geology: huge boulders are still being unlocked by the natural forces of frost, wind and tide to plummet furiously down to the shore, providing the developing habitat for colonising plants. The cliffs have served as a refuge for thousands of

---

years for communities of plants and birds, while major changes have destroyed their habitat further inland.

Along the base of the undefended cliffs grow many rarities, nourished by salt spray, such as rock samphire, golden samphire and curved hard grass. Many lichens survive in the unpolluted air, delineated in clear zones of grey, orange and black, according to their tolerance to salt. The wild or sea cabbage grows here, just as William Turner found it in 1548: 'at Dover harde by the seasyde, it groweth much in rockes and cliffes.' Once it was cut and sold in the market at Dover for a range of claimed medicinal properties, from curing headaches to preventing drunkenness.

The cliffs contain a series of sediments lain down during and since the last Ice Age. To geologists studying the development of the British Isles these sediments are a vital data bank of information, the recognised reference which they use to define the subdivisions of geological time when they date sites elsewhere in Britain.

This is one of the finest undeveloped stretches of coast in England. It is doubly celebrated – as a piece of Heritage Coast, nominated by the Countryside Commission, and as part of the Kent Downs Area of Outstanding Natural Beauty, designated in 1968 under the 1949 National Parks Act as an area whose outstanding scenic quality merited special protection.

The cliffs are the abrupt edge of the scarp of the North Downs, a landscape of singular nobility which contains many rare natural riches, living and fossilised. This is a comforting countryside of soft rounded forms. Behind the steep south-facing escarpment is an undulating landscape, deeply dissected by a series of dry valleys, intimate natural enclosures smoothed by melt-waters during the Ice Age. The steeper slopes of the valleys and escarpments have never been ploughed, and the rich chalk grasslands are a living museum of flowers. These grasslands have been naturally managed over centuries, grazed by sheep and rabbits to check the emerging scrub which would blot out the more delicate species.

This is true downland scenery: chalk grassland, light coloured, rough textured and gently rolling. Once this habitat stretched in broad bands of open downland across Kent, but much was submitted to the plough to grow corn during the Napoleonic Wars around 1815. The Downs have been steadily claimed for agriculture ever since. Today only 700 hectares of unploughed, unimproved chalk grassland remain in Kent, much of it around these cliffs.

Here the insular British wildlife takes on a European dimension: this is England's nearest point to the Continent, and species occur here which are otherwise absent or very rare in Britain – the early and late spider orchids, the Kentish milkwort with its delicate blue leaves, and the Nottingham catchfly, a slender perennial herb whose fragrant flowers open at night when it is visited by insects and bumble-bees. A plant of dry slopes, rocks and cliff ledges, it is abundant around Shakespeare Cliff and Abbot's Cliff.

These high cliffs are a famous landfall for migrating birds and insects, some on the edge of their breeding range like the Kentish plover, previously thought to be extinct in Britain, and the elusive Savi's warbler.

Among eighteen species of butterfly found here is the rare Essex skipper, with its quick, darting flight. There are two moth celebrities, the fiery clearwing and straw belle, both delicately poised on the edge of survival in England and recorded in the *Red Data Book*, which lists Britain's most threatened species.

On the gault clay behind the cliffs is Biggins Wood. This is an ancient woodland – the term describes woodland which has grown continuously on the site since 1600 and probably earlier, a habitat under constant threat. It contains field maple and an area of elm, now almost extinct in southern England. Under their cover flourish the indicator species of old woods, such as the early purple and butterfly orchid and twayblade.

The Channel Tunnel, linking England and France, is to be drilled at a point near Folkestone. If it goes ahead, it will be one of the largest construction projects ever undertaken in Europe and it is likely to result in a great and cumulative environmental impact on the Kent countryside, with the sinking of the tunnel and the construction of roads, railway yards and massive terminal facilities. Damage will be inflicted upon the precious area of coastline between Folkestone and Dover and there will also be major consequential developments elsewhere in the country, with new warehousing and industrial pressures. CPRE has been leading much of the environmental defence, inside and outside Parliament.

View to the north from Summerhouse Hill. Much of the tunnel infrastructure will be situated nearby

Summerhouse Hill close to the Pilgrim's Way behind Folkestone

Summerhouse Hill with Folkestone in the distance

Shakespeare Cliff where spoil from the tunnel workings will be dumped

Beachborough Pond with Summerhouse Hill in the background. The area will be drastically and permanently scarred when the Fixed Link infrastructure has been built

AN AUSTRALIAN COMMERCIAL PHOTOGRAPHER WORKING IN LONDON,

Graeme Harris HAS ALWAYS REGARDED LANDSCAPE PHOTOGRAPHY

AS A HOBBY · IN RECENT YEARS HE HAS DEVELOPED AS AN EXPERT IN THE

FIELD AND HAS SPENT MANY MONTHS WORKING IN OXFORDSHIRE

ON THE EFFECTS OF THE EXTENSION OF THE M40 MOTORWAY

The essence of the serene English agrarian landscape can be traced to a point close to the centre of England. There is a gap in the escarpment, north-west of Banbury and south of Stratford-upon-Avon, between Edge Hill and the miniature range of the Burton Dassett hills. The Warwickshire plain slips through here to form a wide, level, unspoilt vale, about a mile and a half across, neatly finished by steep flanks. This is a supremely untroubled countryside, the enduring peace in the basin of the valley disturbed only by the sound of tractors, bird-song and cows. The rural picture has been frozen for 200 years, apart from some minor evolution in the cluster of small hillside villages.

On the edge of Farnborough village stands the Hall. In an act of landscaping genius and with a profligacy at which later ages can only wonder, the hall was fused inextricably with its setting, the valley. The original landscape concept of Farnborough Hall embraced the entire valley. For over 200 years the hall's broad curving terrace walk, three-quarters of a mile long across the valley, has afforded some of the most voluptuous aspects from any of England's stately houses. There is the view over the mile and a half to Warmington on the other side of the valley; then there is a second broader prospect which unfolds with the walk, north-west, three miles up the valley towards Edge Hill. Once the Holbech family, who owned Farnborough Hall, held the whole of the valley and could create whatever landscape they liked. Today the hall, a Grade I listed building six miles from Banbury, is owned by the

---

National Trust. Now the property and the view are open to anybody.

Farnborough, which was originally called Fernberge, or 'little hill of the Ferns', is all thatch and yellow stone. In the church is a memorial to a Holbech, who was Bishop of St Helena, and the grave of an unidentified tramp who was given comfort in the village. In the Domesday Survey the Bishop of Chester is recorded as holding most of the land around the village. The manor was granted to the Say family in the early Middle Ages. In 1322 it was sold to John de Rale, or Raleigh, thought to be from the same Devon stock as the great Elizabethan, Sir Walter Raleigh. It was passed in 1683, after the slump in the financial fortunes of the Raleigh family, to the local Holbech family from Mollington, two miles to the south. Ambrose Holbech bought the manor in 1684 for £8,700.

A later Holbech, William, began the reconstruction of the old manor-house of the Raleighs. After his grand tour in Europe between 1730 and 1745, which inspired him with a love of Italian art and architecture, he remodelled the house on the lines of a Palladian villa. He collected paintings by Canaletto and Panini and ancient sculpture to incorporate into the decorative schemes of three splendid rooms, whose rococo plasterwork is some of the finest in Britain.

But it was the great terrace walk designed by Sanderson Miller that sets the hall above many such houses of similar history and architectural quality. The earliest record of the terrace comes from the antiquary John Loveday who remarked that he 'rode on Mr W. Holbech's terrace' in 1742. The herculean undertaking was celebrated by the poet Richard Jago in 1767: 'In sturdy troops the jocund labourers hie ... A thousand hands smooth the slanting hill.' There is a touching story of how William Holbech used to walk along the terrace in the morning to greet his brother, Hugh, who was lord of the manor of Mollington.

A gentle curve leads the visitor past a series of viewpoints where the developing spectacle may be savoured. Half-way along is the Ionic temple. The visitor may pause here to behold a patchwork of fields and hedgerows stretching into the blue hazy distance 'providing a quintessentially English scene', notes the National Trust guidebook. The end of the terrace is marked by a pleasing, slender obelisk, with a viewing platform. By the end of the terrace the visitor is almost half-way across the valley, with panoramic views over the Warwickshire plain beyond Edge Hill, where Charles I and Prince Rupert faced the Parliamentarians on 23 October 1642 in the first big battle of the Civil War, towards Stratford-upon-Avon and the Malvern Hills.

A few alterations were made to the house in the nineteenth century, but the house and garden remain largely as they were conceived 200 years ago. The hall belonged to the Holbech family until 1960, and the family still lives in the house.

Warmington village, built on the escarpment facing the valley, sits snugly in a hollow beneath its church. It is one of the most attractive in Warwickshire, built around a spacious triangular green. Being an important part of England's historic landscape, it has been designated by English Heritage as an area of outstanding historic interest.

After ten years' controversy and a public inquiry, the Government has finally approved plans for the building of the M40 motorway, through a corridor of largely unspoilt countryside between Oxford and Birmingham. CPRE led much of the opposition to the insensitive route chosen by the Department of Transport – and won some concessions. But the motorway will still pass along the length of the Warmington Valley, damaging the incomparable landscape around Farnborough Hall.

Burton Dassett Country Park near Warmington, Warwickshire

TOP *Frosty fields near Edge Hill, Warwickshire*
ABOVE *Winter scene, Burton Dassett Country Park, Warwickshire*

top *Doddington Hill near Warmington, Warwickshire*
above *Misty spring morning near proposed M40 route, Warmington Valley*

Late summer cornfield near Warmington

BERKSHIRE · *Newbury*

Helen Harris IS BASED IN BATH WHERE SHE LECTURES PART-TIME

IN PHOTOGRAPHY AT THE BATH COLLEGE OF HIGHER

EDUCATION · SHE IS AN EXPERIENCED AND SENSITIVE

EXPONENT OF LANDSCAPE PHOTOGRAPHY AND HER WORK HAS BEEN

EXHIBITED IN MANY GALLERIES IN LONDON AND THE WEST COUNTRY

Newbury is a dignified old town on the edge of the first piece of relatively undisturbed countryside away from the built-up western fringe of London. On the western side of the Berkshire town there is a tranquil slab of lowland which contains, in a distance of about four miles, all the rich variety of the English countryside – downland, heath, ancient woodland and river valleys. This landscape serves as a visual aperitif for one of the most extensive and least spoilt downland tracts in southern England, the North Wessex Downs Area of Outstanding Natural Beauty, 675 square miles of glorious open countryside.

Newbury's position in the Kennet Valley, south of the steep Berkshire downland, made it a vital point on the western approach to London. Routes by water, road and rail were threaded through the valley. It became one of the finest and most important old towns on the old Bath road out of London, patronised by fashionable processions down to the West Country spa.

Complementing the old road to the west, superseded by the M4 motorway six miles to the north in the 1970s, the Great Western Railway drove its main line to the south-west along the river Kennet. Even earlier the Kennet and Avon Canal linking the Thames to the Avon was built through this gap.

The Romans had a garrison in Newbury. Later Alward, a Saxon thane, built a hamlet of fifty houses there. The Normans came to this tight, strategic valley and defended it with a castle. Two Civil War battles were fought for its control, in 1643 and 1644. On Wash

---

Common, a mile south of the town, are the burial mounds of those killed in the first battle. The second battle revolved around Donnington Castle and Shaw House, to the north of Newbury. Donnington Castle, built in 1386, was devastated by the Parliamentary onslaught. Only the tall and beautiful gatehouse survives: it stands today as defiant as when Oliver Cromwell had finished with it. To the south-west is Donnington Grove, a house of reddish-grey brick built in 1760, standing in a parkland of beechwoods.

Snelsmore Common, to the north-west of the town, is an area of heathland, the largest in Berkshire, containing valley mire and ancient broad-leaved coppice woodland. The common is a wildlife area of European importance, and one of the first in England to be designated as a Site of Special Scientific Interest, in 1955. The valley mire or bog is an uncommon type of heathland – most heaths are dry and well drained. It contains a number of rare species such as bog cotton-grass, bog asphodel and heath spotted orchid.

This low, open common is the haunt of England's only lethal snake, the adder. The tree pipit is found here; so is the nightjar, a declining bird of the dusk and the night, more often heard than seen, with its strange song carrying far on a calm summer night.

Further south is Bagnor, a pretty village by the attractive Lambourn, a bright, pure chalk stream, and Rack Marsh, a meadow enclosed between the north and south channels of the stream, with its rare marsh and meadow species, ragged robin and marsh valerian. This is one of a number of riverside meadows on the Lambourn still relatively unspoilt but now increasingly threatened by drainage and agricultural improvement.

The line of an old railway, now an undisturbed corridor for butterflies and orchids, runs down from here for a few miles over the Hampshire border past The Chase. This is a tranquil 137-acre wood owned by the National Trust. It was left to the Trust by a local landowner, Sir Kenneth Swan, with the request that it be managed as a haven for birds.

The wood is a place of peaceful memorial: it contains a plaque to the memory of Swan's friend, the naturalist Anthony Collett who lived between 1877 and 1929. All three British woodpeckers, the greater-spotted, lesser-spotted and green woodpeckers have been seen there. There is a record of a crossbill, a seed-eating bird with a fierce overlapping beak.

The Department of Transport proposes to reroute the A34 Southampton to Oxford trunk road to the west of Newbury, cutting through its delicate and beautiful fringe of countryside. The new dual carriageway road would sever the south-east corner of Snelsmore Common, the most valuable part of this important heathland, and would run alongside The Chase, permanently shattering its tranquility. Apart from damaging a priceless landscape and wildlife habitat and disturbing the area of the two battles of Newbury, the road would attract developers to the green open space between the road and the present boundary of the town.

Wild roses at the edge of a field at Common Farm. The bypass will cut straight across the foreground

Early morning at The Chase, an area of beautiful and valuable woodland which will be devastated if the Newbury bypass is built

ABOVE *The Kennet and Avon Canal. The road will cross the canal at this point, creating a wide and livid scar across the landscape*
BELOW *Footpath to Donnington Castle at the north end of the proposed route*

ABOVE *Young silver birches on the old railway line to the north of The Chase*
BELOW *Farmland to the west of Newbury. The road would pass diagonally across this field and would be visible for many miles*

DORSET · *Furzey Island*

A HIGHLY SUCCESSFUL COMMERCIAL PHOTOGRAPHER WORKING IN LONDON,

Christopher Joyce *HAS A PARTICULAR FEELING FOR THE*

COASTAL AREAS OF BRITAIN · HE HAS PRODUCED LANDSCAPE STUDIES

FOR HIS OWN ENJOYMENT FOR A NUMBER OF YEARS AND

BRINGS AN ORIGINAL AND INDIVIDUAL STYLE TO HIS WORK

Just west of Bournemouth, on the bustling south shore of England, there is a narrow break in the coast a mere few hundred yards wide. Behind two sandy spits the land pulls crazily back into a line as irregular as unravelled wool, the only break in many orderly miles.

Geological accident has produced great natural riches on this Dorset strand. Most of the different types of coastal habitat found in Britain are represented here, jumbled into the fifty-two miles of indented shoreline which lie within Poole Harbour. There are many little bays, reed- and marsh-covered mud-flats, sand-flats and shingle beaches. Dunes mark the narrow mouth of the bay and to the south is an area of chalk cliff.

Down the centuries the bay has been the secure base of Iron Age man; it has been settled by the Romans, scoured by Viking longboats; it has held the front line in Henry VIII's defences and served as a hide-out for elegant Edwardian society. Today it is recognised as one of the most eminent coastlines in Europe, and its quiet mud-flats attract large numbers of birds.

Poole Harbour is one of the largest natural estuarine harbours in England. It is a sheltered waterway, vast and pitted, shaped after the Ice Age when the post-glacial rise in sea-level flooded the lower Poole basin. Swollen rivers from as far away as Dartmoor carried down sands, gravels and clays from the west, producing the distinctive heathland of the islands and harbour shores.

Man has sheltered in these bays, inhabited these islands and worked these waters for millennia. Recently a dredger found two large timber sections, part of a strong Iron Age log boat, one of the most technically advanced recovered in Europe, preserved for 2,500 years in the harbour silt.

In AD 43 the Roman Emperor Vespasian's armies conquered the local tribe, the Durotriges, using the low-lying peninsula of Hamworthy on the mainland as a supply base for the great legionary fortresses inland. Locally made cooking-pots and jars were supplied to occupying forces as far north as Hadrian's Wall.

Viking longboats regularly swept into the harbour to put the whole of Wessex into terror. King Alfred's fleet rid the harbour of the invaders once, but they returned in 1015 under Canutus the Dane, later King of England, in revenge for the killing of his sister, to devastate the surrounding countryside and lay waste the little chapel on Brownsea Island. Later the island, the biggest in the harbour, carried one of Henry VIII's defensive blockhouses, built just inside the harbour entrance to dominate the deep-water channel against the threat of action by the Catholic rulers of Europe outraged by his rejection of their faith. Owned by a succession of rich and eccentric people, Brownsea is now in the care of the National Trust. Here in 1907 Baden-Powell held his experimental boys' camp, which led to the setting up of the Boy Scout movement.

Poole Harbour is part of the Purbeck Heritage Coast and Area of Outstanding Natural Beauty, awarded a Council of Europe Diploma in 1984. The whole of the harbour is a Grade 1 Site of Special Scientific Interest, listed as one of Britain's 750 élite nature sites in the *Nature Conservation Review*. A product of the harbour's remarkable geography is a double high tide twice a day, a major peak and an echo before the sea finally surges out. This curious tidal cycle optimises the exposure of the feeding-grounds, increasing the amount of available food.

The harbour is internationally famous for its wintering birds which feed and shelter on the mud-flats, reed-beds and salt-marshes. Two species, the shelduck and black-tailed godwit, exceed one per cent of the West European population in Poole Harbour. The numbers of a further seven species, the redshank, ruff, teal, pintail, shoveller, red-breasted merganser and Canada goose, amount to more than one per cent of the British populations.

Some of the most ecologically sensitive parts of the bay are around and to the south of Brownsea and Furzey Islands, a few hundred yards apart near the mouth of the harbour. Furzey, marked with a tall western edge of cliffs, is twenty-six acres of deciduous and coniferous woodland, interspersed with open lawns, laid down in the 1930s when the island was inhabited. Furzey's salt-marsh fringes are important bird havens. Its southern shoreline is a roost for oyster-catcher. The remote and complex topography and diversity of feeding-grounds on the south shore of the bay are particularly attractive to overwintering waders and wildfowl.

Behind this southern shore of the harbour is Studland Heath, a priceless relic of Dorset heathland, which echoes to the dry machine-like trill of the nightjar as it hawks moths over its open spaces at dusk. The very rare Dartford warbler, cocking its long dark tail, skulks in its stands of European gorse. This is a bird always in danger of withdrawing forever to its Mediterranean strongholds. Near the harbour mouth Brands Bay attracts such visiting rarities as Slavonian grebe, with its dark slanting cap, smaller than the native great-crested grebe.

There are red squirrels on both Brownsea and Furzey Islands, survivors of the local populations which have disappeared since they were introduced by man. This is the original British squirrel, much shyer than the now dominant grey squirrel, freezing when man approaches. Few people see it in southern England. One of the rarest of British moths, Blair's pinion, is on Brownsea. So are the declining white admiral, and the bee hawk moth, feeding on the honeysuckle.

Since 1979 oil has been produced at Wytch Farm from the Bridport Sands reservoir, 3,000 feet below Poole Harbour. On the southern side of the harbour oil was first discovered in the mid-1970s. Now British Petroleum has been given permission to drill for oil on Furzey Island, a particularly sensitive area. There is major controversy about the route of the new pipeline proposed by BP for transporting the oil eastwards towards London. An oil spill on the open water could have a devastating effect on this natural harbour.

PAGES 79 TO 83 *Beautiful Poole Harbour, a peaceful and unique haven for bird life and one of the largest natural estuarine harbours in England*

NORTHUMBERLAND · *Druridge Bay*

FROM HIS STUDIO IN EDINBURGH, *Stephen Lawson*

PRODUCES EVOCATIVE AND SPECTACULAR PANORAMAS USING PHOTOGRAPHIC

MONTAGE TECHNIQUES · MANY OF HIS STUDIES SPAN AN ENTIRE DAY

DEPICTING THE CHANGES IN LIGHT AND CLIMATE FROM DAWN UNTIL DUSK

To the north of the heavily populated and badly despoiled sprawl of Tyneside there is a miraculously pure sweep of open sandy coastline. Seven miles long and sand-dune backed, Druridge Bay is a glory to the eyes and a thrill to the senses after the throng and toil of the industrial north-east. The wonder is in its size and the absence of man-made interference. It is a bay of psychological boost and great optimism, whether the visitor stands in the teeth of a furious, unchecked north-easterly gale or on a day of dead calm as the tide creeps in across the sand.

The reputation of Druridge Bay as a wildlife habitat, so close to Tyneside, is widely known. It is one of the most popular sites in the north-east for the bird-watcher. Its bird visitors, pausing on epic flights from the Arctic to the warm Mediterranean, are meticulously recorded.

The bay leaves the industrial smudge behind at its southern end and runs from Snab Point in a slow and leisurely curve with nothing to its north but the promise of unblemished coast all the way to Scotland. It ends at Hauxley Head and the bird reserve at Coquet Island. Around the head are Amble and Warkworth, site of Harry Hotspur's castle. In the far distance the Cheviot Hills emerge, grey and misty, from the flat land.

This is a coastline of passage, to men as well as birds. At Chibburn Preceptory, behind the dunes, a group of the Knights Templar of St John of Jerusalem, a military order of monks, used to provide protection and assistance to pilgrims passing on their way to the Holy Land in the north. A hospital at the village of Druridge was used for the same purpose. In 1313 it was an important group of buildings, 100 yards square, moated with a chapel, hall and living-quarters. It fell into disuse after it was suppressed by Henry VIII, but the site survives.

James VI of Scotland, the future James I, enjoyed the hospitality of Widdrington Castle, in a village behind the Bay, the seat of the Widdrington clan, on his journey to London after the death of Queen Elizabeth I in 1603. He was impressed by the wealth of game in the deer-park. There was a settlement at Widdrington, Wuduhere's farmstead, as early as AD 547.

One day in 1691, the hamlet of Druridge suffered a momentous, if brief, invasion out of that huge beach, when French sailors stole ashore to set fire to the community and raid Widdrington Castle, on to Chibburn Preceptory, and back to their boats loaded with booty. All but one of the raiders escaped.

Coal-mining has come as close as it dared to this famous coastline. Ten million tons of coal lie below the shallow soil behind the dunes and under the sea. Mines run out under the bay, and huge open-cast drifts have been gouged into the shallow soil. Much of the torn-up land has been restored. The long history of mining in this region has produced a bonus for nature. Where the soil has sagged over the subterranean works swampy flashes and shallow lakes have formed to produce important refuges for wildlife. Cresswell Pond, which lies behind the dunes, connected to the sea by the Blakemoor Burn, is a vital refuelling stop in autumn and spring for many long-distance migrants, between the Canadian Arctic, Greenland, northern Scandinavia and northern Russia and their wintering-grounds in southern Europe and Africa.

The slightly brackish water of the pond, a mixture of fresh and salt water, makes it attractive to many species, including the rare garganey, a tiny duck with a flash of white above its eye, the only water-fowl which visits Britain from Africa and Spain to breed, rather than to escape the bitter northern winter. In the last survey, in 1981, only forty-nine breeding pairs were recorded in Britain. The pond gives shelter to sea ducks and waders driven off the sea in severe weather. It supports an uninhibited, raucous assembly of whooper swan, scaup and smew, a duck which breeds in Siberia and overwinters in eastern England.

Cresswell is a raw, untended site: it is remarkable that it retains its wildlife with no official guardian. Naturalists know nothing like it as a piece of spontaneous wildlife habitat between Aberdeenshire in the north and Norfolk in the south. This massing of wading birds attracts birds of prey to the area. Sparrow-hawks and merlins regularly hunt over the foreshore, and the peregrine is a regular visitor. The barn-owl, a species declining as a result of modern farming practices, is seen over the dunes. At the northern end of the bay there are bird populations of international importance, including red-throated, black-throated and great northern divers. Many other small birds also make landfall on this part of the coast, including large flocks of blackbirds, fieldfares, redwings and thrushes. Others passing down the mainland of Europe, caught in adverse weather and swept off course, find rest and shelter here, including tiny warblers from Central Europe and Asia.

The National Trust has bought ninety-nine acres of dunes and grass hinterland, along a mile of coastline in the middle of the bay, using funds from Enterprise Neptune, its coastal appeal. There is a rich variety of flower, insect and bird life on the chalk grassland.

The magnificent Druridge Bay is one of the Central Electricity Generating Board's proposed sites for a new generation of nuclear power-stations – like a number of other remote rural or coastal sites, which the Board has earmarked for such development around England and Wales. At the 1983–85 Sizewell public enquiry, CPRE argued in detail for alternative, less contentious and less environmentally damaging patterns of energy investment.

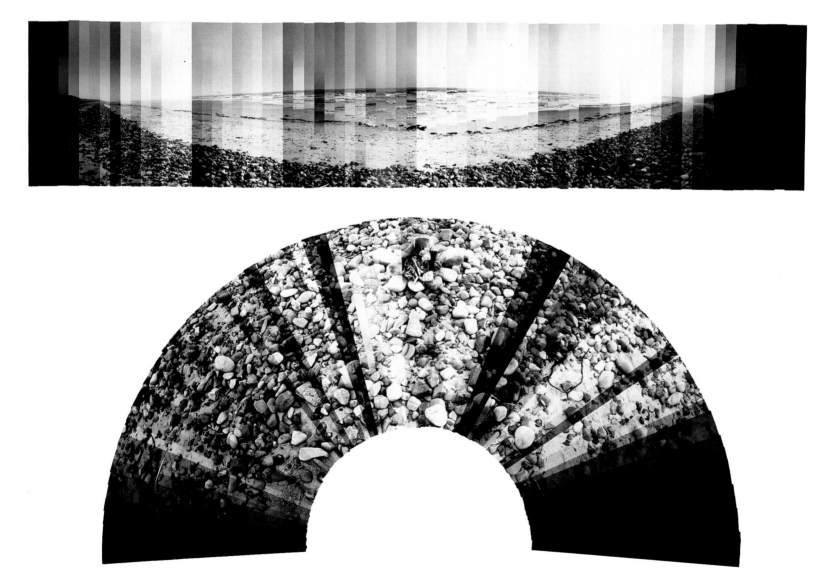

Flood tide at noon, Druridge Bay, Northumberland.
(Strips 3° wide photographed at 9-minute intervals from first to last light)

Druridge Bay in winter, photographed at intervals of $7\frac{1}{2}$ minutes

TOP *The bird sanctuary at Cresswell Ponds, Druridge Bay*

ABOVE *The dunes and sea-shore at Druridge Bay*

AN INTERNATIONALLY FAMOUS PORTRAIT, FASHION AND

LANDSCAPE PHOTOGRAPHER, *Patrick Lichfield* HAS BEEN

PASSIONATELY INTERESTED IN ENVIRONMENTAL ISSUES FOR MANY YEARS ·

HE IS A LONG-TIME MEMBER OF THE COUNCIL FOR THE PROTECTION

OF RURAL ENGLAND AND HAS BEEN INVOLVED IN MANY OF THE

CONSERVATION ISSUES AFFECTING HIS NATIVE WARWICKSHIRE

The name of Hawkhurst Moor calls across dim centuries like the lonely screech of the hunting harrier. In that precise, functional medieval way the name explains the place. Here a hawker trained his fierce birds to work the open land in the great Forest of Arden which Shakespeare described. The moor was first recorded in 1275 as Le Hauekerismore – the moor or marsh of the hawker. By 1553 it had evolved into Hawkersmore. Today Hawkhurst Moor Farm is a well-tended mixture of arable and pasture land in a thin salient of the Green Belt, only six miles wide, that prises apart the swarming suburbs of Coventry and Birmingham.

To the west of Hawkhurst Moor is the village of Berkswell with its white-walled cottages and its stout, timbered houses. The origins of this community can be fixed half a millennium earlier than the moor, to the very beginnings of English history. In 772 the Saxon abbess St Mildred is said to have been buried in the parish church. Traces of Saxon masonry survive in the crypt of the present Norman structure.

Berkswell's Saxon foundations also lie in its name. It means literally 'the well of Bercul' or 'Beorculu', who owned the well in a forest clearing in which the monks of Lichfield baptized the King of Mercia. The well still exists as a sixteen-feet-square stone-lined pond. The last

---

Saxon connection was with 'one Levant' who owned land in the parish before the Norman invasion, after which it was conferred 'with a great profit' to Robert, Earl of Beaumont.

From then on the trail of Berkswell and the surrounding land is well signposted through history. The Domesday Survey records that Berkswell was in the Coleshill Hundred of Warwickshire, and that Beaumont owned a woodland a league long and a league wide, five hides (a hide was a unit of land of about 120 acres) and land for eight ploughs, together with villagers and servants.

The manor of Berkswell can then be traced through the Earls of Warwick, the Crown, through the Morrowes and the Eardley-Wilmots, one of whom became a governor of Tasmania, and finally to the Wheatleys. From 1550 onwards the village's history is recounted in the extravagant detail of wills and inventories, parish registers, court rolls, hearth tax returns, glebe terriers and the accounts of churchwardens, constables and overseers of the poor.

Many lesser tourist sites are more celebrated than Berkswell, an oversight which should not concern the discerning visitor. It is one of those reticently charming places basking in a well-practised tranquillity. There is a long pedigree in its buildings and environment. It is the essence of a village that has grown and evolved over 1,200 years, with ancient, well-preserved buildings and its encircling system of old tracks and paths.

The church of St John the Baptist, one of the finest examples of Norman and Early English architecture in the Midlands, dates from the twelfth century – the most interesting Norman church in Warwickshire, in the opinion of Sir Nikolaus Pevsner, the great authority on English architecture. Its traces of earlier Saxon stonework are an unusual feature for a smaller parish church. In a room above the south porch is a Russian flag bearing a double-headed eagle. It was brought home from the Crimea by one of the Eardley-Wilmots. The church has a half-timbered vestry and a listed stone cross, which may have been either a market cross or an ancient preaching cross.

The stone well of Bercul, whose waters reputedly have healing powers, is close to the church beside the imposing seventeenth-century rectory, the Well House. It feeds the lake in the park of Berkswell Hall, a proud place flooded with rhododendrons as spring merges into summer.

The village is rich in old buildings. The centre is a conservation area containing forty-one Grade II listed buildings. Many were erected between the mid-sixteenth and the beginning of the seventeenth centuries when the wealthy village was growing rapidly, with 'a great rebuilding' of homes for rich and poor. There are red-brick Victorian almshouses and the surviving black-and-white timbering and thatch of village-centre buildings. One half-timbered cottage contains a tiny museum. The sixteenth-century Bear Inn used to take its beer from the Malt House, standing opposite.

On the village green there is an eccentric memorial to public ridicule, a set of five-hole stocks. The odd hole is reputedly to accommodate a one-legged recalcitrant. There is an old windmill which last ground corn in 1948.

The antiquity of the village is complemented in the ancient fields which contain it, presenting an unbroken prospect of green to people leaving Coventry. There are many ancient hedgerows on Hawkhurst Moor, with oaks and ashes from the same stock as the trees of the old Forest of Arden. These hedges are unremarkable compared with officially designated nature habitats, yet they sustain the indispensable species of the common English countryside, such as the white-throat, yellowhammer, partridge; and the butterflies – meadow brown, speckled wood, small copper, small tortoiseshell and comma.

Where the good farmland gives out nature floods in. On Rough Close sixty-two different species of plant have been recorded, including sphagnum moss. The Tile Hill Wood is a local nature reserve and a Grade I Site of Special Scientific Interest. Part of it is ancient woodland, haunt of the smooth newt and the great-crested newt, an itinerant creature which strays many yards from its home pond.

At Cornets End sand and gravel workings have been transformed by time in a delicate network of pools, silt lagoons and marshland, with alder wood and fields of herb grasses. Here eighty-four species of flora are recorded, as well as thirteen species of butterfly and four of dragonfly. This is the breeding-site for great-crested grebe, little-ringed plover, ruddy duck, reed-bunting and the drought-hit sand-martin.

So close to two large cities, Coventry and Birmingham, and so vulnerable, these fields and these parishes of Berkswell and the adjoining Burton Green with their population of 3,300 people could easily have been sucked into suburbia. Local people are in no doubt that their continuing physical independence is due to the Green Belt, an enduring corner-stone in planning policy which maintains cordons of green around large towns and cities.

Hawkhurst Moor is the site proposed by British Coal for a massive new coal-mine from which it intends to extract three million tons of coal annually. The siting of a coal mine here in prime Green Belt land, which was intended to remain undeveloped as a buffer between built up areas, would have a massive impact on a beautiful and placid rural environment. It would destroy a number of important nature habitats and shatter the abiding peace of Berkswell and neighbouring villages. Alternative ways of exploiting the coal seam, through more remote access, are being explored by CPRE and other bodies.

TOP *The Village Stores, Berkswell*

ABOVE *Bluebell Wood, close to Southurst Farm*

TOP *The village blacksmith at Berkswell*
ABOVE *Swans on the lake at Berkswell Hall*

TOP *Field near Berkswell, close to the proposed spoil dumping site*
ABOVE *Field near Berkswell, site of the proposed spoil tip*

TOP *Berkswell Hall*
ABOVE *Skipping race during sports day at Berkswell village school*

Children playing in a cornfield on the site of the proposed NCB site at Berkswell

ESSEX · *Bradwell on Sea*

A NEWCOMER TO THE PHOTOGRAPHIC SCENE IN ENGLAND,

Jenny May IS A SUPERB LANDSCAPE PHOTOGRAPHER · SHE IS

ALSO KNOWN FOR HER STYLISH PHOTOGRAPHS OF BUILDINGS AND

NATURAL PATTERNS · JENNY LECTURES ON PHOTOGRAPHY IN LONDON

At the end of Essex, where the flat land slopes into the grey North Sea, there is one of the earliest Christian buildings in England. For 300 years St Peter's Chapel stood as a barn, after men had forgotten its function. It was reconsecrated in 1920 and it stands today, very simple, tall and beautiful, a solid block of masonry against its huge background of field, marsh and open sea, and the destination of many pilgrimages. It grew, as many of England's oldest churches did, out of the stones of an earlier building. Before it was erected by the pious men from the north, the Romans set their guard here against the marauding sea rovers.

For such a remote place the sparse land around Bradwell is remarkably rich in historical association. Just up the river Blackwater from here the Danes slipped ashore in the second week of August 991 to fight a battle which is one of the earliest recorded in the English language. Bradwell is today a quiet village of weather-boarded houses at the end of a road, on the edge of the Blackwater estuary. The wind is constantly about it, bending the reeds and billowing the rusty red sails of the preserved Essex barges, re-enacting their traditional progress up the river.

The site of the great third-century Roman fort Othona, or Ithancaster, is hard up against the sea. Carausius, one of the counts of the Saxon shore, built it as one of a line of nine defences between Norfolk and the Isle of Wight. Once it covered six acres and was 520 feet long with walls 12 feet thick. The sea has claimed most of it. When the Empire expired, some older Romans stayed to work the land around the peninsula, the Dengie Hundred. The abandoned stones from their great fort were reused to build the chapel of St Peter on the Wall. The church is the most completely preserved of the earliest group of churches in England, associated with the seventh-century reintroduction of Christianity into the south from its stronghold in the north. It was set up in 654 by a monk from Lindisfarne, St Cedd, the brother of St Chad. Since he was also a bishop, this has been described as the oldest cathedral in England. Later William the Conqueror gave the building to the monks of St Valéry in Normandy. The apse was lost; its curved outline can still be seen in the grass to seaward.

For many years the nave's firm profile served as a beacon to early sailors. It fell into disuse: for 300 years it was a barn, but this common function saved it. In 1920 people remembered how famous and sacred this ancient place was. It was so carefully restored that few would know that the twentieth century had touched it.

In August 991 a huddle of swift Danish boats slipped past the chapel and sailed up the estuary of the Blackwater. They occupied Northey Island, upstream from Bradwell, attached then, as now, to the mainland by a 400-yard causeway. The Saxon Brihtnoth, the Ealdorman of Essex, kept them trapped on the island, then with commendable but misplaced honour let them on to the mainland to engage in fair fight. He lost his life in the subsequent Battle of Maldon. A Saxon survivor wrote a remarkable account of the battle in *The Anglo-Saxon Chronicle,* one of the first-known histories in the English language. The original manuscript was burnt in 1731 but by good fortune a copy has survived.

There is more boisterous history connected with Bradwell Lodge, a Tudor house at the south end of Bradwell village. This was the seat of the outrageous, high-living cleric Sir Henry Bate Dudley, who also entertained himself, and others, as a journalist, a gallant and grand host in this house.

Bradwell and its hinterland are now protected behind a sea-wall, anxiously scanned for invasion by the angry sea which boiled over this countryside in 1953. At one time the marshes around Bradwell supported 1,000 sheep, which grazed around thirty decoy ponds on to which wildfowl were lured to be shot for the London table. Today the defended land is given over to crops: the natural riches start beyond the straight north-to-south line of the two-yard-high dyke. This is Dengie Flats – a sweep of saltings, a diminishing habitat nationally, merging into an expanse of mud.

The Dengie Flats is a distant, little-visited place, undisturbed in winter, the whole area exposed to the tide and the savage easterly winds. Close to the sea-wall in the shingle and mud are rare local plants, the shrubby sea blite and lax-flowered sea lavender.

Up to a quarter of the world population of dark-bellied Brent geese gathers on this Essex coast in the winter, one of the largest concentrations of intertidal mud in Britain. This clean, safe mud is a vital link in a chain of natural feeding-stations for migrating birds at the bottom of the east coast.

There are several national nature reserves within the Blackwater estuary, with its inlets and winding creeks, a calmer place away from Dengie's vicious winds. There is a national nature reserve at Old Hall Marsh, a Royal Society for the Protection of Birds reserve at Tollesbury Wick, and an Essex Naturalists Trust reserve on Northey Island, owned by the National Trust.

Bradwell is one of the nuclear industry's new research sites for the possible dumping of low-level nuclear waste. Naturalists fear that there could be contamination to the internationally important bird havens in the Blackwater estuary and on Dengie Flats. There is also the risk of a sea flood invading a site of buried nuclear material and releasing radioactivity over the land. The peace of Bradwell and the string of villages on the only road leading into it would be permanently broken by the ceaseless transporting of nuclear waste over many years to come, if the area was selected as the final location for such waste disposal.

Wildflowers growing free on unsprayed land at Bradwell, Essex

Bradwell Bird Observatory, perched on wooden stilts above the marshes

RIGHT *Old hide near Bradwell Bird Observatory*

BELOW *Shutters on the Bird Observatory at Bradwell*

ABOVE *Signs of Bradwell's local opposition to nuclear dumping*

LEFT *Wildflowers on the marshes at Bradwell*

St Peter's chapel, close to the edge of the village where the marshland begins

SUSSEX · *Fairlight Headland*

Linda McCartney STUDIED PHOTOGRAPHY AT UNIVERSITY

IN AMERICA AND SOON DEVELOPED A REPUTATION FOR FINE PORTRAIT AND

REPORTAGE WORK · SHE HAS PUBLISHED SEVERAL BOOKS ON HER

PHOTOGRAPHY AND HAS RECENTLY HELD TWO SOLO EXHIBITIONS

AT THE ROYAL PHOTOGRAPHIC SOCIETY · LINDA IS EXTREMELY

CONCERNED WITH THE FATE OF THE ENGLISH COUNTRYSIDE AND IS CLOSELY

INVOLVED WITH THE FIGHT TO PROTECT THE AREA WHICH SHE RECORDS HERE

On the hectic, built-up coast of Sussex there is a glorious, undeveloped gap in the smother of concrete to the east of Hastings where the land steps up into a high clay cliff above pebbly coves and tight, plunging valleys. Spread upon this promontory is a steep tract of heathland, trees and hedges. In spring a carpet of wild flowers rolls away to the north and a vivid patch of bright yellow gorse lights up the cliff edge at Fire Hills.

Out to the east is the lonely flat spread of the Pett Levels and Romney Marsh, a place ill at ease with the sea which has choked its harbours and strangled its ancient commerce. No tide comes to Winchelsea now, unquestionably inland but once a prosperous port, or to the charming town of Rye.

To the west, before Eastbourne and Beachy Head, is England's most famous battle-site. William the Conqueror came ashore just down the coast at Norman's Bay, the other side of Bexhill, and hurried four miles inland to take his decisive victory over Harold in the Battle of Hastings, on Senlac Hill at Battle on 14 October 1066.

All this is visible from the summit of Fairlight Down, North Seat, which at 595 feet dominates its landscape. It is the highest point between the South and North Downs and the second highest point in Sussex, after Crowborough. To the north the famous Sussex woodland surges on to the horizon; to the south, on a clear, slack day of low soft sun, the coast of France beckons dimly, forty-five miles away across the Channel. Fairlight Down is the emphatic southern conclusion of the High Weald, a slab of sandy ground forty-seven miles wide by nineteen miles deep, bounded by the chalky South Downs of East and West Sussex and the North Downs of Kent and Surrey.

The High Weald, an Area of Outstanding Natural Beauty which takes in Fairlight Down, presses tightly up to the edge of Hastings. It is a landscape of great variety, a series of flat-topped or gently rounded ridges separated by broad valleys, occasionally cut by streams and rivers and drenched with trees. Some of these shaws and copses of oak, ash, beech, birch and holly may be the last relics of the great southern forest of Andredsweald.

Down to the sea, off the watershed on Fairlight Down, run the narrow valleys known as the glens of Hastings – Fairlight Glen, Warren Glen and Ecclesbourne Glen. These are tight, densely wooded habitats with their distinctive microclimate, supporting plants normally found only in western Britain. On the eastern flank of the Down lies the old village of Fairlight. Its church, on the crest of the hill, serves as a landmark to the boats fishing the waters close to the coast. Fishermen line up a coastal marker with the church tower and home in on their fishing beds to within twenty feet.

The cliff edge of Fairlight Down is an area still undergoing a violent change of identity. As recently, in geological terms, as 1287 there was a massive collapse of these cliffs along a fault line at a time of violent storms. The tidal drift began to choke navigable waterways to Rye and Winchelsea in the marshy lowland to the east. Edward I devised a new planned town at Winchelsea, but the verdict of the sea was irreversible and navigation was never restored.

Hastings was a famous old port, one of the original Cinque Ports. It, too, was deceived by the sea which clogged and closed it. Once it was cut off from the rest of England by the impenetrable swamps of Romney Marsh on the east, the Pevensey Levels on the west and the uninhabited clay forest of the Weald to the north.

There is evidence of Iron Age settlement at Hastings. Later it was occupied by the tribe of the Belgae. It was their support for Julius Caesar's Gallic enemies that was one reason for Caesar's invasion of Britain in 55 BC. Hastings Castle was built by William the Conqueror's man Robert, Count of Eu, together with a church where St Thomas à Becket was dean. The timber fort which pre-dates it was William's first construction on English soil. He set his administrative base here.

The comparative isolation of this coast ended in the nineteenth century when the opening of the railway brought the Victorian middle classes steaming down to a brisk new environment. They took care never to spoil Fairlight Down. Without its diligent defenders it could so easily have been submerged in some tasteless turn of the century development, some folly of Edwardian exhuberance. But the down survived, as a rare vantage point from which to reflect on the busy ebb and flow of history over this coastal region, and from which to observe the evolution of the intricate pattern of the southern landscape. It is a place to stand above England and pause.

Recent seismic surveys of the geological structure under Fairlight Down indicate that there may be oil reserves there. An oil company has applied for planning permission to drill an exploratory borehole, and recent experience in on-shore exploration in southern England suggests that there is a good chance of oil being found here. The application to drill was rejected by the local council, but the oil company has the opportunity to appeal to the Government. Exploration and any subsequent extraction, involving the building of highly conspicuous handling and transport facilities, would be a major intrusion into a prominent and highly scenic landscape.

PAGES 107 TO 109 *Impressions of Fairlight Down on the coast, high to the east of Hastings, where oil exploration is a serious risk*

The Somerset Levels

ONE OF THE WORLD'S GREATEST REPORTAGE PHOTOGRAPHERS,

Donald McCullin HAS RECORDED MANY OF THE GRIMMER ASPECTS OF

RECENT WORLD HISTORY · HE LIVES CLOSE TO THE LEVELS IN SOMERSET

AND FEELS PASSIONATELY ABOUT ENGLAND'S COUNTRYSIDE

Out of the flat fields of the Somerset Levels and Moors floats the ancient whisper of a landscape surviving beyond its time. The horizon retreats over a primitive patchwork of rectangular wet pastures enclosed by lazily draining rhynes, ditches waymarked by tottering lines of pollarded willows. It is a relic of a barely remembered form of agriculture, thousands of years old; it is a land sparing to the farmers who tend it, but unstintingly generous to the nature which still overwhelms it.

It is a dramatic, lonely monochrome place by winter with big skies reflected in the flooded fields, under great wheeling flocks of wildfowl, drawn across hundreds of miles of frozen England by some instinctive inherited certainty. By summer its meadows, under a gentle discipline of grazing and haymaking, are a blur of unrestrained flowers and darting birds. The electric blue of a dragonfly illuminates an old rhyne. On a still spring evening the bubbling song of a curlew lies in the dense air, to the counterpoint of a piping redshank and strangely drumming sound of the snipe. With infinite discretion an otter plops into the water.

Naturalists set this place above any other wetland in the country. It is a relic area, a living display of what parts of England were like hundreds of years ago. Species which were once common but are now otherwise confined to a few marshes in Kent and part of the Norfolk Broads are found here in profusion. Nowhere in England are there tracts of flower-rich meadows to match these strange, dishevelled, tussocky places. Some of the meadow plants growing today, ragged robin, kingcup and marsh orchid, can be traced genetically to species found in peat laid down 5,000 years ago.

The moors and levels cover 250 square miles, hemmed in on three sides by the Mendip, Blackdown and Quantock Hills to the north-east of Taunton and north-west of Yeovil. These are, strictly speaking, two separate habitats, totalling about 140,000 acres: the levels are recent clay deposits between a point two miles east of Bridgwater and the sea. The moors are areas of inland clay, overlain by peat formed from the decaying of the vast inland fenland.

Prehistoric man built his villages on the islands in the lake. Meare and Glastonbury are among the most important Iron Age sites in Britain. Archaeologists have found here one of the most complex systems of prehistoric trackways in Europe, timber boardwalks linking the islands which stood above the flooded land. By the end of the fourteenth century sea-walls were built to exclude the tides allowing land to be cultivated. In 1800 further attempts were made to restrain the five rivers, the Axe, Brue, Huntspill, Cary and Parrett, and their tributaries which meandered aimlessly out of the hills and into Bridgwater Bay.

Of the original area of levels and moors about twelve per cent retain their high wildlife importance as pristine grazing marsh untouched by the ravages of intensive agriculture. On the best areas, such as South Lake Moor, farmers continue an ancient practice of deliberate flooding, by opening a sluice on the river. Flooding enriches the land with red water, a cocktail of top soil, silt and nutrients from the surrounding high ground.

Once this winter flooding covered much of the levels with up to three feet of water. Those areas which are still flooded attract huge numbers of wintering birds. There are vast flocks of widgeon, pochard, tufted duck and golden plover from Scotland and Scandinavia. Snipe can be counted in congregations as large as 6,000 around one pool on Kingsmoor. Bewick's swans home in unerringly every winter from their Arctic fastnesses to the same few fields. In the early spring the rich damp feeding-meadows are a refuelling stopover for whimbrel migrating north to Iceland and Shetland.

Cattle are excluded until late spring when the ground nesting birds have hatched. Haymaking is delayed until flowers – meadowsweet, yellow iris, angelica and pepper saxifrage – have already set their seeds. A typical field may hold more than forty species of grass, compared with two or three under the heavy hand of agriculture. In the summer yellow wagtails move up from Africa with winchat and sedge-warbler which nest among the taller plants alongside the rhynes.

These rhynes, a peculiar, enclosed habitat which performs a rudimentary drainage for the moors and provides an open barrier to cattle, are remarkable corridors of sanctuary for wild creatures. The old method of hand cleaning, with rakes and knives used to cut and pull out weeds, encourages a diverse range of flowering plants. Over the deeper waters there are floating species, such as duckweeds and frogbit; on the shallow edges are water-violet and bladderwort.

The most spectacular plants are those which grow in the shallow water, and flower tall above it – bulrushes, sedges, the great water-dock, water-mint and marsh horsetail. One of Britain's rarest dragonflies, the variable damselfly, is found in the rhynes. They contain two other great insect rarities, the hairy dragonfly and ruddy darter. Many rhynes are bordered by pollarded willows or osiers, their wood still used in basket-making, for charcoal and cricket bats. They are home to a whole community of wild creatures, from tunnelling beetles to owls, redstarts, tree sparrows and grey herons.

The Nature Conservancy Council (NCC), the Government's nature agency, has identified 18,000 acres of the levels on a list of the élite sites in Britain, in the updating of its *Nature Conservation Review*. Over the past few years the Council has been buying land in the levels in an attempt to stop them being improved and to prevent the loss of their wildlife interest.

The NCC owns or leases large parts of the levels, where traditional benign management continues, with the encouragement of the Government. But there has been a rapid march towards a more intensive form of agriculture over much of the rest of the Somerset levels and moors. Farmers have drained wet meadowland, reducing the water table in order to grow cereals and other profitable crops. This has destroyed irreplaceable wildlife over much of this unique landscape. Some farmers are proposing to end the centuries-old tradition of annually flooding the land, which could lead to further drainage. In other places the grasslands have been drained and reseeded and treated with herbicide and fertiliser to give a better grass yield for cattle. These improved grasslands do not support the flower and bird life which was previously found upon them. The rhynes become polluted with chemicals running off the land, and the new regime of cutting their vegetation annually by machine destroys their aquatic vegetation and insect life. There has also been a huge increase in the winning of peat, used mainly for gardening, during the 1980s: peat winning further destroys habitat and leaves water-filled hollows which are worthless to nature.

ABOVE *Stormclouds over Sedgemoor*
OVERLEAF *View across the Somerset Levels to Glastonbury Tor*
PAGES 116 AND 117 *Wetlands under a heavy sky at Sedgemoor*

NORFOLK · *Halvergate Marshes*

A SPECIALIST IN PHOTOGRAPHIC ESSAYS OF RURAL SUBJECTS, Garry Miller

LIVES IN LINCOLNSHIRE AND HAS HELD MANY SUCCESSFUL

EXHIBITIONS OF HIS WORK IN LONDON AND EAST ANGLIA ·

HE IS CLOSELY ASSOCIATED WITH THE ENVIRONMENTAL MOVEMENT AND

MUCH OF HIS WORK IN THIS AREA HAS BEEN PUBLISHED IN RECENT YEARS

The authentic Norfolk Broads, that part still undamaged by the bow-wave of the motor cruiser, are private and subdued, overwhelmed by the huge East Anglian sky. It is a low, uncrowded landscape containing only a few spare details: a high flock of wintering geese wheeling in off the sea, a scattering of derelict windpumps, old dyke gates, browsing cattle. On the distant valley sides there is an enclosing fringe of woodlands and hedges.

The variety of habitat and visual quality of the Broads makes this one of England's most important landscapes, celebrated in the nineteenth century by the Norwich School of Painting. It contains the largest remaining blocks of fens – low, wet, marshy land – in Britain. This apparently simple countryside has an intricate construction: wide expanses of water fringed with reed and silvery willows and carr woodland are divided by dykes, picked out with margins of water lilies, and slow-flowing rivers.

Many rare species cling to survival here. It is the last refuge in England for the swallowtail butterfly, which lays its eggs on the milk parsley, a Fenland plant. The rare Norfolk aeshna dragonfly darts precisely along the marsh dyke system. The water-soldier is a plant unique to East Anglia, its stem submerged with its hard serrated leaves standing in correct military order above the still waters.

Much of this landscape and habitat has, ironically, been developed under man's hand. The Norfolk Broads are a relic of one of the earliest forms of fuel production. They are created from the lower valleys of the Waveney, Yare and Bure, and the tributaries of the Bure, the Ant and the Thurne, which drain two-thirds of Norfolk and much of north Suffolk. The Broads are shallow lakes which originate from peat diggings excavated in medieval times when the region fuelled the fires of East Anglia. After the thirteenth century a gradual rise in sea-level flooded the pits, creating a watery, indented landscape unique in Britain.

There are numerous surviving devices of these ancient waterways – restored wherries with their single huge arm of sail to catch the merest breeze. Once these boats plied between remote staithes – landing-places where they would unload coal, cereals and people. At these same staithes craft would have delivered consignments of stone from Caen in Normandy to be used to build the larger churches. In earlier times the lack of stout stones dictated the architectural style: Saxon towers were built round, in split flint, so no corner-stone was needed.

Buildings and settlements are an important part of the Broadland scene. Some relatively undeveloped villages, such as Ranworth and Belaugh, illustrate the ancient pattern, with buildings grouped around the parish staithe, the common, ferry or bridge.

Halvergate Marshes, 6,000 acres of open grazing-land west of Great Yarmouth, are the heart of the traditional Broads. The village of Halvergate sprawls about the edge of the wide open space of the marshes. Where the Yare flows into Breydon Water is the railway station of Berney Arms, so remote it seems to serve no destination other than itself. Occasionally a train saunters in from the world beyond. Here is the High Mill, the tallest windpump in the country, with its boat-shaped cap and white sails.

The expanse of grazing-meadow between the Bure and the Yare has escaped much of the change which has swept over the English landscape in the past 200 years. This marshland was once sea estuary, reclaimed by the digging of drainage ditches. Sea shells are still turned up as evidence of its maritime origins. As the land started to dry out, it shrank and became lower than the level of the sea. To prevent flooding the banks of the river were built up. Boats on these elevated waterways now seem to sail above the land.

The drainage of the Broads was achieved through a complex network of interconnecting drains and dykes, cut into the fen, through which water flows to the rivers. There are 16,000 acres of drained marshes around the Broadland rivers, formed before the eighteenth century by the embanking and drainage of estuarine mud-flats. At one time the water ran away by gravity, with sluices to prevent the sea water flooding back on high tides. In the seventeenth century windpumps were installed to control water-levels more effectively. By the nineteenth century there were more than 200 windpumps in operation. They are all redundant now but remain important features of the landscape, dramatic lonely sentinels.

In the dykes tradition conspires on behalf of wildlife. In Halvergate, where farmers still keep their grazing herds on the land, the dyke water is unaffected by the fertilisers which have seeped off the land and poisoned other waters on the Broads, and a regular flow of good clear water sustains a rich and diverse plant life. By grazing the sides of the dykes cattle keep down the tall grass which would crowd out more delicate species: by treading down at the water's edge as they drink they create a ledge, a micro-habitat for wildlife.

The shallow grazing marsh dykes are a living repository of virtually all the plants and most of the related animals lost to many of the Broads. These species have retreated to the dykes as their former habitat was destroyed by agricultural improvements. In the future scientists may be able to draw on this natural storehouse to restore the fauna of the Broads when their turbid waters have been cleaned.

The dyke system contains 100 species of aquatic plants, two-thirds of the water species found in Britain. They include the water violet with its lilac, yellow-eyed flower, the frogbit, the arrowhead and the decorative and lethal carniverous bladderwort, which traps small water creatures. The bittern, a shy, elusive bird prowling these watercourses for fish, frogs and toads, is betrayed by its strange and mighty booming call, echoing across the empty Fens.

Traditional harvesting for marsh hay has kept the fens open and has favoured the rarities they support: on these areas of waterlogged, spongy, peaty soil grow the flowers of meadow enchantment – fen orchids and broad buckler-fern, white meadowsweet and yellow marsh marigolds. The carr woodland, dense wet tangles of undergrowth on the edge of the Fens, is marked by the huge form of the greater tussock sedge, which grows to a yard wide at its base, and the yellow flag iris, with its tall, sword-shaped leaves.

The Broads are a vital sanctuary for birds. The Halvergate Marshes in winter are a feeding- and roosting-area for 300 Bewick's swans. But this is no random stopping point for birds travelling hopefully. Each autumn of their long lives, Bewick's swans depart from the Soviet Arctic when the first glaze of frost touches their home lakes and set their unerring course across 2000 miles for this flat, secure place. There is recognition for its international importance for nature conservation in its designation under the 1971 Ramsar International Wetland Convention.

The open marshes are the territory of some of our sharpest aerial hunters – barn-owls, kestrels, hen-harriers and short-eared owls. These unblemished and extensive tracts are critical to their survival. To a bird such as the marsh-harrier, now down to no more than a few dozen nesting pairs in Britain, the balance of habitat is quite perfect – reed-fen areas for nesting, close to extensive reed areas for feeding where this low-level hunter performs its glide-and-pounce technique. The dykeside and rough boggy meadows, with their grassy tussocks, are havens for mute swan, shoveller, oyster-catcher, lapwing, redshank and yellow wagtail. This is a stronghold, too, of the bearded tit, which has retreated here as reed beds elsewhere in England were cleared and wetlands drained. Like many of our prime rarities, it needs a quick eye to spot it, flitting over the reeds and dropping quickly from view. But its prominent moustache-like tufts, offering a wealth of facial expression, make it a species unmistakable to those lucky enough to see it.

The entire landscape of the Norfolk Broads faces continuing pressure from a more intensive form of farming. Much of the previously untouched fenland has been drained, ploughed and treated with fertiliser and turned over to wheat and barley production. This process has entirely destroyed the value of the fens for wildlife and suffocated its remarkable landscape. Even lands which have so far escaped improvement are at risk from the run-off of herbicides and fertilisers applied on adjacent fields. Drainage ditches, with their specialised wildlife communities, have also been polluted by the spread of agricultural chemicals.

A new government scheme to help farmers maintain traditional agricultural practices was introduced recently, following successful pressure by CPRE and other bodies, offering a degree of safeguard to those few places in the Broads, like Halvergate Marshes, which have so far remained largely unaffected by change. But the threat to this highly vulnerable landscape remains.

ABOVE *Wild meadow flowers in abundance on* Halvergate Marshes
OVERLEAF *Dramatic East Anglian cloud formations over* Halvergate Marshes

DORSET · *Winfrith*

A WELL KNOWN AND INNOVATIVE FREELANCE PHOTOGRAPHER,

Alistair Morrison SPECIALISES IN PORTRAITURE

AND LANDSCAPES · A COMPARATIVE NEWCOMER TO THE ART, HE IS BASED IN

MIDDLESEX BUT TRAVELS WIDELY WITH HIS MOBILE STUDIO

'Singularly colossal and mysterious in its swarthy monotony.' That was Thomas Hardy's description of Egdon Heath in *Return of the Native*. Egdon Heath, by any reading of the map, is Winfrith Heath in the west of Dorset, a rearing bank of vivid purple heather, splashed with the creamy yellow of the prickly, low-growing western gorse.

Hardy superimposed Egdon on Winfrith, placing it above his invented Wellbridge (the real village of Wool) below his King's Bere (Bere Regis) to the north-east and his Casterbridge (Dorchester) to the north-west. It is his description of Winfrith whose atmosphere charges the opening pages of his book. 'The plan is perfectly accordant with man's nature, neither ghastly, hateful nor ugly, neither commonplace, unmeaning nor tame, but, like man, slighted and enduring.'

Winfrith, a few miles north of the furrowed Dorset coast, is a buffeted remnant of a sweep of heathland which once covered much of the coarse sandy soil of the south coast, and which has contracted still further under the assault of agriculture since Hardy died in 1928. What remains is highly prized. Winfrith has been nominated as one of the élite wildlife sites in Great Britain. This is one of the last strongholds of the Dartford warbler, persecuted by frosts and the deep, burning heath fires but thriving in the places which most closely imitate its preferred Mediterranean territories.

This is a landscape of great age – 'From prehistoric times as unaltered as the stars overhead,' wrote Hardy. In the Bronze Age there was a thin cloak of oak and birch over this heathland. Early farmers cleared this cover for low-grade agriculture but they were defeated

---

by the inherent poverty of the soils, extremely acidic and low in nutrients, and a deterioration in the climate. Unwittingly they had created a tract of mean, open beauty. This heathland became the predominant vegetation in this part of Dorset and the New Forest. Two hundred years ago there were more than 90,000 acres in Dorset: that total has been dissected and trimmed so that today only about 12,000 hectares survive. Of these remaining patches Winfrith is the most westerly.

The dark mystery of Winfrith is captured in music. Hardy is believed to have taken the composer Gustav Holst over the heath when it was November-brown and forbidding. The author was frail and had only two years to live. Holst was inspired to write his tone poem *Egdon Heath* which he dedicated to Hardy. Holst was moved by the haggard landscape and tried to reflect the desolate picture which Hardy had conveyed in *Return of the Native*. He wrote the piece during the summer and autumn of 1927. When he was half-way through the work he went to Dorchester to visit the ailing Hardy, who was looking forward to hearing the music. Ironically Hardy died in January 1928, only three weeks before its first performance. According to his daughter, Imogen, in her biography of the composer, Holst considered it his best work.

Holst's *Egdon Heath* is dark, intense music subtitled 'A Homage to Thomas Hardy'. It is written for full orchestra and has one movement. The slow-moving music is fixed in a *pianissimo* hush, with half-muted strings depicting the vast, empty heath and remote woodwind chords conveying the solitude by night of Rain Barrow, a burial-chamber of some great chieftain from the far past.

To the naturalist this is a wonderful but incongruous piece of undisturbed ground, surviving against the bitter logic of agricultural improvement. Winfrith contains the full range of heathland habitat – dry knolls surrounding a depression with valley bog in the bottom and wet heath intervening, flecked with marsh orchids and heath spotted orchids. Man has exploited it, but with restraint, cutting gorse and peat for fuel and bracken for bedding. These low demands have maintained its delicate balance where no species can be allowed to overwhelm its neighbour.

The heath contains many of the rare creatures associated with Dorset heathland: reptiles such as sand-lizard and smooth snake; the stonechat, tree pipit and nightjar. That neat swift hawk, the hobby, hunts over its tight confines. The silver-studded blue butterfly flits low and dainty over the light purple flowers of the cross-leaved heath. The marsh gentian, with its fluted blue flowers, a very local declining plant with most of its population on Dorset heathland, is here. Another is the marsh club moss, a scarce southern heathland plant, and the bog orchid, an uncommon flower found mainly in the north with outlying populations here, poised delicately on the edge of extinction.

The Nature Conservancy Council lists Winfrith in its *Nature Conservation Review* as one of the 750 most precious sites in the country. Because this habitat is so fragmented, what is left at Winfrith must be sustained in its present size, about 500 acres. As it diminishes, it becomes less able to recover after the devastating fires which afflict it. And recolonisation by its specialist species, arriving by hazardous routes over sterile farmland from the other outposts of heathland, becomes more difficult.

The Central Electricity Generating Board has chosen land on the edge of Winfrith Heath as a possible site for a nuclear power-station. Because it is an inland site, any power station there would need four massive cooling towers. These would overwhelm the Dorset countryside for miles around, dwarfing the small research station on an adjacent site and changing the entire character of the area.

PAGES 127 TO 129 *Aspects of Winfrith Heath, Dorset – a unique and precious habitat for wild flowers and wintering birds*

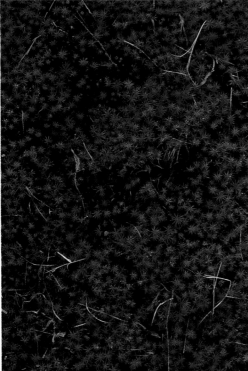

CURRENTLY SPECIALISING IN GARDENS AND LANDSCAPES,

Cressida Pemberton-Pigott HAS HELD

SEVERAL EXHIBITIONS OF HER WORK · SHE RECENTLY COMPLETED AN

EASTERN ARTS COMMISSION ON EAST ANGLIAN WATERWAYS · HER REAL

LOVE, HOWEVER, IS THE LAKE DISTRICT, WHERE SHE WAS

BROUGHT UP AND WHICH SHE HAS RECORDED WITH GREAT SENSITIVITY

'Persons of pure taste throughout the whole island, by their visits to the lakes in the North of England, testify that they deem the district a sort of national property, in which every man has a right and interest who has an eye to perceive and a heart to enjoy' – William Wordsworth, *A Guide through the District of the Lakes* (1835).

The Lakes are unmatched in England as an area of accessible, concentrated magnificence, with stupendous, sharply rising mountains complementing intense waterside beauty. The region's associations with painting and literature, architecture and poetry have given it a unique status. It is one of the few British landscapes to be short-listed as a world-heritage site. It is where the British national park movement was founded, where the National Trust set root, and where the sport of rock climbing took its first grip in the 1880s.

The 880 square miles of the Lake District National Park, wild moorland and boulder-strewn peaks, penetrated by sparingly farmed valleys, was designated a national park in 1951. Many people consider it to be Britain's leading national park. It is certainly the biggest; it has the most varied scenery; it perfectly conforms to the concept of the national park, 'an extensive area of beautiful and relatively wild country in which, for the nation's benefit, the

---

characteristic landscape beauty is strictly preserved' (*Dower Report*, 1945).

Each valley derives a particular character from the rock types through which it passes. Each is separated from its neighbours by high intervening watersheds. There are distinct hillside features: lines of oak, beech and ash flowing down to a lakeside, or forming a huddle to shelter farm buildings; casual fringes of alder, birch and rowan tracing the ghylls or gullies, with their silver threads of water. It is the English landscape in harmony with the men and women who live and work in it. Man's influence as a farmer extends up the hills to the in-byes, the ancient pasturages traditionally marked off in stone from the bleak scree and wild moorland above. There is a deep and continuing respect for the landscape: national park aesthetics demand that the whole complicated stone tapestry of field boundaries be re-erected if it falls down.

Visitors in the mid-eighteenth century first recognised the pastoral perfection of Lakeland and saw in it the subject-matter of the Classical Arcadian landscape, representing idealised happy country life. Elizabeth Bennet in Jane Austen's *Pride and Prejudice* exclaims to her aunt Mrs Gardiner, on the subject of a proposed visit to the Lakes: 'What delight, what felicity. You give me fresh life and vigour.'

Thomas West, in one of the first guides to the Lakes, identified viewpoints or stations from which visitors could gaze upon a composed prospect of lake and hills. But it was Wordsworth more than anyone else who communicated the beauty of the Lakes to a wider audience, evoking the now widespread concern for the conservation of the landscape.

Windermere, on the east of the region, was the closest and most easily discovered destination for these new visitors. But Derwent Water, to the north-west, was to many the finest of the lakes, girdled by ancient broad-leaved woods under the dramatic ridge of Maiden Moor and Cat Bells in the west, and in the east the cliffs of Falcon and Walla Crags, and the brooding might of Scafell Pike. At the southern end the silver chain of the River Derwent tumbles off the fells at the top of Borrowdale.

Thomas Smith, who made his engraving of Derwent Water in 1761, wrote: 'the beautiful lake near Keswick in Cumberland; 'tis more than ten miles round, finely diversified with rocks, woods, islands in some parts about fifty fathoms deep.' The first property which the National Trust owned in the Lakes was at Brandel How on the north-west shore.

Ruskin said the view from Friars Crag above Derwent Water was one of the three most beautiful in Europe. He records that one of his first memories was being taken to the crag where he remembers seeing the exposed roots of trees, a common sign of erosion in Lakeland. Today his monument is there. The artist J. M. W. Turner rowed on Derwent Water. Thomas Gainsborough and John Constable and many others took inspiration here. In another form of homage the monks of Lindisfarne came to the shrine of St Herbert on an island in the lake.

Hugh Walpole, one of the most successful novelists of his time, moved to the Lakes in 1924 to a house at Brackenburn on Derwent Water. He set his four *Herries* novels, passionate romantic sagas, around the close huddle of cottages beneath Watendlath Fells. His characters came and went in the woods and fells around the river Derwent and the Borrowdale Valley.

Appropriately for a place of literary achievement, the area was in the past famous for pencil manufacture, based around graphite deposits in the Borrowdale Valley. One of the great environmental battles fought by Canon Rawnsley, a founder of the National Trust, was that in which he successfully resisted proposals to drive a railway line along the north shore of Derwent Water to serve the mines. Canon Rawnsley first aroused the nation to the dangers that threatened the Lake District in the nineteenth century. The Trust bought its first property in 1902. The Trevelyan gift in Langdale Valley in 1928 established the Trust as a major Lakeland landowner. Another considerable benefactor was the writer of children's books, Beatrix Potter.

The Trust now owns the most scenically memorable quarter of the Lake District National Park, nearly all the central fell massif over 1,000 feet and the important valley heads, as well as 85 farms, more than 250 houses and cottages, 23 lakes and tarns, and many woodlands and areas of shoreland. Access costs visitors nothing and is entirely unrestricted on the uplands. The guardians of the Lakes strive to maintain its purity, in its natural habitat and its ancient man-made structures. The National Trust is progressively removing the alien larch and replacing it with the natural sessile oak, which once smothered the lake's shores, on the eastern bank of Derwent Water.

In an attempt to restore its properties in the most seemly way the Trust is reaching back into an age of almost forgotten craftsmanship. Its craftsmen repair farm buildings in traditional lime mortar. Burnt lime is slaked in a bath, mixed with river gravel and two sorts of sand. This covering is flexible, porous and absorbs water. The sun dries it like a cloth. This process is longer lasting and provides a better damp-proof than cement rendering and paint. And instead of sawn timber, used for the past eighty years on barns and house roofs, which rots quickly and lacks internal strength, the Trust's craftsmen are reviving the use of oak and ash, split along the grain, taken from its own coppices at Borrowdale. The process is more labour intensive and expensive than the use of sawn wood but it is historically correct, lasts a lot longer, and looks much better.

There is constant pressure from house developers to build along the shores of Derwent Water and other lakes. Although a recent plan to build holiday chalets and a conference centre close to Derwent Water at Keswick was overturned, the area is under continuing threat.

ABOVE AND PAGES I34 AND I35 *The beauty and tranquillity of the lakes exemplified by the breathtaking splendour of Derwent Water*

DEVON · *Dartmoor*

ONE OF OUR GREATEST AND MOST RESPECTED PHOTOGRAPHERS,

Snowdon IS BASED IN LONDON · ALTHOUGH HE IS

CELEBRATED IN PARTICULAR FOR HIS SENSITIVE AND

EVOCATIVE PORTRAITS, HE HAS A STRONG

FEELING FOR THE BRITISH COUNTRYSIDE

Dartmoor is the most accessible wilderness in southern England. It rears up as a compact 365-square-mile island of high ground, studded with granite tors, gnarled outcrops of great age, with their shadow of tumbled boulder fields. It offers its visitors 100,000 open acres without the impediment of a wall or human detail.

The moor, one of England's ten national parks, is set above a sweep of shimmering farmland, stretching north through the green and fertile distance to the Bristol Channel. Two thousand farmers, who extract an uncertain living from the ancient heath, share it with eight million visitors a year. Travellers will note from a great distance its brooding and remarkable heights, the closest approximations to mountains south of the Pennines.

The moor is a place for enterprise and discovery. For the army, who lodge on it and enact real combat, it is as rugged a habitat as any in the world of potential conflict. For the young there is the challenge of rapid treks between high tors; for the rambler of any age serene walking.

Dartmoor satisfies because it is compact, not vast or complicated like some of England's other wild and grand places. The challenge is not of perilous rock-faces but of wide open space with low profiles and very few landmarks. Its subtleties of slope and perspective can confuse even those who know it well. The initiated admit to the shock of meeting an apparently freshly hewn jumble of boulders or some unexpected variation in the direction of a stream.

It is a gentle, balmy place compared with the north. The winters are not as hard as the Pennines or Lakeland, although in its most savage disposition Dartmoor is a place of overwhelming violence, of rain or snow and tempest. But there can be just as intense an effect on the perceptions in a swirling autumn mist as in the spring when the larks are singing and the buzzards and golden plover are working the lonely wastes.

Bronze Age farmers first created the moorland as it is today by clearing the mantle of trees between steep valley sides and blanket bog. The husbanded fringe of Dartmoor has ebbed and flowed for centuries as reeves and moormen have managed Dartmoor Forest – the medieval designation of hunting terrain belonging to the monarch. Stumps of oaks found in blanket bogs 1,700 feet up suggest that there was once an ancient cloak of woodland.

Generations of farmers have conquered, surrendered to and reconquered its thorny fringe, their progress encouraged and deterred by the oscillating impediments and stimulus of Black Death and Corn Laws, and, more recently, EEC incentive. One force alone prevents the moor from reverting to a medieval thicket – the chomping power of a vast army of sheep whose attentions restrain the merging scrub and let the autumn heather thrive.

On its northern flank Dartmoor points a rugged shoulder at Okehampton. The national park begins and ends here. This market town is contained between the high, desolate wilderness above, and docile pastures below. It is on fringes such as these that a striking geographical transition – moorland and fields and villages and sullen tors juxtaposed – allows people to believe themselves in a wild place while they cling to lowland security.

The engineers of the Southern Railway led their line around the moor through the woodland above the town, respecting its powerful contours, except when they broke out in a noble viaduct over the river Okement where it spills busily off the high ground. Today only the passage of huge consignments of quarried stone sunder the calm of this delicate place. When they have passed, the silence of the moor descends like a cloak.

Above the town, and within the boundaries of the national park, is Okehampton Park, a medieval deer-wood which slopes down from the bare heights of Dartmoor. It contains a rich succession of history, the prehistoric Halstock Camp with its huge banks and trenches, encompassing magnificent views down into the deep wooded cleave of the Moor Brook. There are hut circles, an ancient beech-lined bridleway from Okehampton to Tavistock, and old tinners' workings. On its edge is Okehampton Castle, the thirteenth-century stronghold of the Courtenay family.

At the western end of the park are Bluebell Woods, given to Okehampton Hamlets' Parish Council in 1865 by Mrs Mary Ryan in memory of her late daughter. The trust-deed decrees that the land shall be held 'as an open space preserved for the recreation and enjoyment at all times by the public'.

Kate Ashbrook, secretary of the Open Spaces Society, said of Okehampton Park: 'Places like the park are vitally important not only for those who are able to visit them regularly, but also for those who like myself are exiled from them or who may never see them but for whom the knowledge that they exist, largely unaltered through the centuries, open and untamed, gives them inspiration, comfort and the secure knowledge that we have not yet sacrificed all to the demands of modern life.'

In 1986 the Department of Transport gave final approval for the building of a dual carriageway trunk-road to by-pass Okehampton to the south of the town. The new road will lace through the northern flank of the Dartmoor National Park, cutting a wide gash across Okehampton Park and bisecting Bluebell Woods, with the loss of many mature trees, and passing close to the ancient Okehampton Castle. The decision to build the road on this route overturns the verdict of an all-party Parliamentary Committee which ruled that the road should be routed outside the park, following a campaign by CPRE, the Open Spaces Society, the Ramblers Association, the Council for National Parks and others.

ABOVE *High Tor on moorland to the south of the route*
OPPOSITE *Misty moorland on the northern edge of Dartmoor, close to the new bypass*

OPPOSITE *Okehampton Castle, which sits immediately to the north of the bypass*
ABOVE *Moorland stream running to the south of the town and close to the new road*
OVERLEAF *Sunset behind a distant Dartmoor church tower*

LEICESTERSHIRE · *Kirby Muxloe Castle*

A BUSY AND HIGHLY COMPETENT COMMERCIAL PHOTOGRAPHER,

Koo Stark *HAS ALWAYS REGARDED HER LANDSCAPES AS A HOBBY · SHE BRINGS*

A SENSITIVE EYE TO THE PROBLEMS OF THE COUNTRYSIDE AND

PLANS TO DEVELOP THIS SIDE OF HER ART

The unfinished ramparts of Kirby Muxloe Castle are a permanent mark of ambition unfulfilled, loyalty spurned and the brutal demands of statecraft. Built by William, Lord Hastings, one of the foremost men of his day, the castle is a monument of national importance. It is one of the finest surviving examples in England of a fifteenth-century brick-built castle; but it was never completed.

The castle stands on low ground near a stream on the edge of the village of Kirby Muxloe, four miles west of Leicester. Although unfinished, it is still an impressive structure, standing 300 feet across, under a large open tract of rising rural landscape to its north-east, now tidily tilled. This buffer of pleasantly rolling farmland was once part of the parkland with which Lord Hastings surrounded his castle, and is now its only open aspect. Standing on this side of the castle, the visitor may easily use its outline to blank out the developed background and imagine the castle more or less as it was when the departing fifteenth-century builders left it, unfinished. Few English castles are as unspoilt by subsequent development around them as Kirby Muxloe, ennobled by the surviving aspect to and from it over open fields. It retains its dignity, even with the houses of the village in the background on the one side and the droning M1 motorway, hidden in a cutting, on the other.

Work was begun in 1480, and the castle soon rose high and confident; but in 1483 Hastings was denounced as a traitor by Richard, Duke of Gloucester, the future Richard III, whose cause he supported, and he was executed swiftly and without ceremony. How did Hastings, described by a contemporary French chronicler as a man of honour and prudence, suffer this undeserved fate? He was a strong supporter of the Yorkist cause in the Wars of the Roses and was closely attached to Richard, Duke of York. He played an important part in the restoration of Edward to the throne after the King's temporary overthrow in 1470, commanding the third battalion in the decisive battle of Barnet in 1471. After Edward's death in 1483 he was considered to be a supporter of the Duke of Gloucester, the future Richard III, rather than of the dead King's widow and her son Edward V; but the duke did not trust him and denounced him.

In Shakespeare's *Richard III* (Act III, Scene IV) the tragedy unfolds thus:

> Gloucester: '... Thou art a traitor.
>> Off with his head!...
>> I will not dine until I see the same.'

Hastings's noble departing words are:

> 'O momentary grace of mortal men,
> Which we more hunt for than the grace of God!
> Who builds his hope in air of your good looks,
> Lives like a drunken sailor on a mast,
> Ready with every nod to tumble down
> Into the fatal bowels of the deep.'

The memory of his supporter, so hurriedly sacrificed, was revived for Gloucester about eighteen months later when, as Richard III, he passed along the old road to the south-west of the castle. Imagine him looking down across the valley towards the unfinished castle, a memorial to mistrust. History does not record his reaction.

The rejection of Hastings is imprinted in the castle, now in the official care of English Heritage. It began as an expression of a high and powerful man, able to indulge his taste in fine buildings. Hastings was a man of great wealth, drawing considerable revenue from his state offices and through marriage. His castles at Ashby-de-la-Zouch and Kirby were built to the same principle – as domestic buildings of moderate defensive strength.

He was enriched with grants of forfeited Lancastrian estates as a reward for services to his good friend Edward IV in the Civil War. In 1474 Hastings was granted a licence to enclose 2,000 acres at Kirby Muxloe and crenellate or fortify the house which already stood on the site. The story of the castle's construction was recorded in exceptional detail in the building accounts, found much later wrapped in leather in a chimney at Castle Ashby, Hastings's main residence. They record the spending of £1,088.17s.6¾d. over four years from 1480 to 1484, from the time of the optimism of a powerful lord to the doubtful days after his downfall.

The master mason, John Cowper, who also worked on Magdalen College, Oxford, and Winchester and Eton Colleges, was well at work for 8*d*. a day by May 1481; under him was Robert Steynforth and itinerant Welsh builders, John and Hugh Powell, and William Griffith. They made a forge to smelt iron and put up wooden hurdles, the medieval equivalent of scaffolding-board. By July the foundations for the walls of the courtyard were being dug and rough-stone foundations for the courtyard were set. A shed was erected, the haven of masons at their refreshment through the ages. In August oak boards were being prepared from which templates were cut as mouldings.

Mr Davy Bell superintended the cutting out of the moat: men were posted to watch the stream at night lest a sudden rise in its level should flood the moat before the banks were high enough. It was completed by September when the dykers' work was done. Straw, fern and hurdles were provided to cover the new walls against the coming frosts. There is a record of prodigious labours from a visiting Fleming, Anthony Docheman, for which he was paid 10*d*. a week. Once he made 100,000 bricks in a week, using seventy-eight loads of wood. In the month before Hastings's demise the men were on top of their job, fitting the lead pipes and gutters. Then, in June, the master lost his head. Uncertainty settled on the enterprise. The bricklayers and masons stopped work at once, the traditional reflex of men worried about their pay packets. They restarted the task in September and carried on in desultory fashion for a year; but their work was never completed.

The castle remained in the Hastings family until 1630. It was given to the nation in 1911, and the repair of the castle and clearing of the moat were finished in 1913. Today, behind its officially defended perimeters, nature is undisturbed. Herons pace through the brook which feeds the moat. In summer kingfishers flash a vivid blue and red over the still waters. Barn-owls hold power in this castle now, in permanent residence in the West Tower, sharing the night hunting with the long-eared bat.

There are features in the surrounding countryside, created by man, which are as old as the castle itself. The road that runs down to Braunston is banked with an ancient hedge which was set in the twelfth century. This was the old coal road between pits at Swannington to the north-west and Leicester, worn down by heavily burdened pack-horses.

A property firm has drawn up proposals to erect as many as 1,000 houses on the farmland next to Kirby Muxloe castle on its north and east sides, its only open aspect, thus totally surrounding it with twentieth-century development. Although the fabric of the building itself would not be damaged, one of Britain's finest unfinished castles would be smothered by nondescript housing and would forever lose that sense of history and nobility which it derives from its open setting.

PAGES 147 TO 149 *Kirby Muxloe Castle, a beautiful and historically important barrier between the countryside and the town*

CAMBRIDGESHIRE · *Ely Cathedral Close*

A FREELANCE PHOTOGRAPHER BASED IN LONDON, Paul Wakefield

HAS WORKED EXTENSIVELY ON WELSH LIFESTYLE AND LANDSCAPES · HE HAS

PUBLISHED THREE BOOKS ON LANDSCAPES IN BRITAIN

AND HAS EXHIBITED HIS WORK ON A NUMBER OF OCCASIONS

IN WALES AND IN THE PHOTOGRAPHERS GALLERY IN LONDON

From a distance of about ten miles in any direction, signposts become irrelevant to the traveller to Ely. Its cathedral stands as a soaring landmark, one of the greatest feats in the architecture of the Western world. It has spiritually dominated East Anglia for hundreds of years and physically commanded the huge fenland of south Cambridgeshire. People still come across the Fens in the manner of a great medieval pilgrimage, with wonder and amazement, drawn to the massive raised form on its island site, hallowed since 673 when St Ethelreda, Queen of Northumbria, first came to Ely.

Once the cathedral, 537 feet long and 215 feet high at the west tower, reared up, grand and remote, above a lake which covered this low swampy ground. The Fens have long since been drained and Ely, a small market town with a population of about 11,000, dignified with the title of city since 1973, has grown in its shadow. But the cathedral has always stood apart; a cordon of open ground has survived to fend off the indignity of building up to its very precincts.

The first church in Ely is thought to have been consecrated by the founder of Christianity in Britain, St Augustine; but its recorded history begins when Ethelreda came to the island to found a religious community in 673. Ethelreda was revered as a saint for her piety and humility at the time of her death and remained one of the most popular saints throughout the Middle Ages.

The Danes sacked the community in 869. It was refounded as a monastery in 970. After the invasion of William the Conqueror, Hereward the Wake put up one of the last stands of the Saxons on the island. He exploited the community's natural watery defences, burning the reed-beds to destroy a causeway which the attackers were crossing. After the surrender of the monks, William installed his own man, Simeon, former prior of Winchester. It was the octogenarian Abbot Simeon who initiated in about 1081 the building work on the cathedral which stands today, using stone from a quarry at Barnack near Stamford in Lincolnshire.

After the collapse of the central Norman tower in 1322, the cathedral's sacrist, Alan of Walsingham, conceived the octagon, built of eight huge pillars. These were crowned with a wooden lantern tower made from twenty oaks, yielding great timbers, as much as sixty-four feet long, which were brought from Chicksands in Bedfordshire. It is a work of engineering genius in any age, a supreme example of medieval craftsmanship.

Over the centuries Ely has lost its isolated status, but it has never ceased to overwhelm its surroundings. On the southern flank there is a glorious cascade of open parkland where cattle graze under the cathedral's noble bulk. The Great Ouse river meanders gracefully along the foot of the hill to the east. At first the cathedral is hidden from the riverborne visitor by buildings. Then, further up the hill, a view of gathering magnificence opens out over the Cathedral Close, a haphazard, unexpected eastern profile with the disordered components of a great cathedral, Octagon, Lady Chapel, St Ethelreda's Chapel and Bishop West's Chantry.

This meadowland to the east of the cathedral has never been developed in the 1,300 years that a consecrated building has existed here, so the cathedral has always stood glorious and unimpaired by lesser building to anyone approaching from the east.

This eastern view has recently been at risk. The Dean and Chapter, needing to raise money to repair the cathedral's associated medieval buildings, proposed building forty-three houses in the two-acre meadow. The housing estate would have closed off forever a most unexpected aspect of the cathedral. But this is the story of a threat averted. The John Paul Getty III Trust is providing the Dean and Chapter with £100,000 a year for five years to carry out the essential repairs with the result that the meadows will not now be developed. The cathedral authorities have now launched a separate appeal to meet the cost of building renovation.

PAGES 152 TO 155 *Autumnal aspects of Ely Cathedral, one of England's most precious medieval buildings*

GOOD·LORD·DELIVER·THEM

The North Pennines

Denis Waugh IS ONE OF THE GREAT LANDSCAPE PHOTOGRAPHERS ·

HE IS BASED IN BRITAIN BUT HAS AN INTERNATIONAL REPUTATION FOR HIS

WORK · HIS STRONG BUT SENSITIVE PICTURES HAVE BEEN

EXHIBITED AND PUBLISHED THROUGHOUT THE WORLD

The North Pennines are a land of extremes. Few areas of England have known greater tempest, such deep and lasting chill, and such profound geological upheaval. It is also a place of unspoilt villages and unsullied perfection in its nature habitat, the last stronghold in Britain for some plants and birds.

This is a landscape of great age, high and essentially horizontal, with graceful changes of gradient, gently sweeping ridge lines and distant horizons. The landscape is vast yet simple: the eye dwells on the rich mosaic of natural vegetation and subtly varying colours, ranging from the silvery white of nardus grass, with its wiry and slender leaves, to the deep purple of heather.

On its fringes the high moor merges into the softer dales, wooded valleys snaking up through them into the cloudy heights. And below them the villages of the Dales, built from stones hewn from their own hinterland. On the western scarp is a string of ancient villages whose parish boundaries, far up the slope, show the limit of ancient farmers' ambition in this severe country.

This is the largest continuous section of land over 2,000 feet outside the Highlands of Scotland, the pre-eminent example of an upland moorland plateau, less modified by man than any area of similar size in England: 860 square miles of remote grandeur, surrounded by national parks, its highest, wildest points linked by an epic route to the north, the Pennine Way. It should, on any objective assessment, have been declared a national park itself, but through historical accident it was never designated when the other parks were established.

The North Pennines are a rectangular block climbing to Cross Fell and Great Dun Fell, the two highest summits in England outside the Lake District. Lines of great geological faults on its western and northern edges mark it out. An alternation of shale, sandstone, limestone and thin coals in sequence give it a stepped appearance. Enormous sheets of molten rock, dolerites, solidified to form bleak, grey landmarks whose very names set them on a remote and distant plane – High Force, Falcon Clints and Cronkley Scar.

Melt-water from glaciers has hollowed out a honeycomb of underground caverns. Two such are Knock Fell Cave on Cross Fell, with its intricate range of chambers and passages, and Fairy Hole Caves in Weardale. In other places the caves have fallen in to reveal dramatic, steep-sided limestone gorges; at God's Bridge part of the collapsed cave roof remains as a natural bridge.

The geological eccentricities, cliffs, screes, gorges, are habitats for a complex intermingling of unusual species. The primeval action of ice and frost and the spring melt have wrought massive changes in the original geological building material; and even today stone still moves under the pressures of freeze and heat. At Warcop some of the exposed limestone laid bare by glaciers has been weathered into pavements.

These pavements, some of the most remarkable geological features in England and protected under Act of Parliament, are found mainly in the Pennines. Their characteristic features are clints – huge paving-stones – and grykes – the fissures or cracks which separate them – etched down by rains over thousands of years. Each gryke is a micro nature reserve, with scattered shrubs of birch, rowan and bird cherry, thought to be remnants of ancient woodlands which once cloaked these inhospitable expanses of rock.

The Pennines are a place of great meteorological excess. Snow lies on Cross Fell for up to 140 days a year, longer than anywhere else in England. On Great Dun Fell plants will grow for only a third of the year – on 129 days. Here, in January 1968, the wind blew with the greatest ferocity ever recorded in England, at 134 miles per hour. And appropriately for a region as apart as this there is a wind which blows only here, the 'helm'. This is a north-easterly, amplified by local conditions, which blasts down the western slopes of the Vale of Eden.

Fauna and flora of the highest importance grace these heights: there are twenty-eight Sites of Special Scientific Interest, two of them national nature reserves. The very top holds species which have survived since the Ice Age. There is a dense covering of blanket bog, with hare's tail, cotton-grass and cloudberry, giving way to richer areas of grassland containing rarer species such as the spring gentian, with its deep blue rosettes.

The North Pennines are of international importance for their bird populations. Nine of the seventy-nine most threatened birds in Britain breed here, including the crossbill and the goshawk. Two out of five of the English population of the merlin, a small declining falcon, find here the conditions which are exactly suited to its specialised hunting routine. The merlin nests in the mature heather moorland, within easy reach of lightly wooded or scrub-covered moorland edge and farmland, where the fortunate may see it expertly flying down a meadow pipit, snatching it on the wing.

The peregrine, whose stoop from a great height on to its prey is one of the most electrifying sights in nature, haunts these lonely hillsides. These are some of the best grouse moors in the world. The blackcock is here in these uplands which contain the largest lek, the display site of this rare game bird. This is the territory of the dotterel, one of only two known breeding-sites in England. In winter it is a feeding-ground for the golden eagle.

In the Upper Dales there are more extensive flower-rich hay meadows than anywhere else in Britain. Here habitats mingle and collide, woodland in the Dales, with small streams tumbling down deep valleys cut into the upland plateau, their lines picked out by sinuous bands of alder, rowan, birch and holly, thickening with oak, ash and wych-elm lower down, with the largest area of juniper scrub in Britain. These are some of the richest woodlands in England, in terms of the wildlife they contain. Many rare plants grow here, such as herb Paris, with its four wide leaves and single yellow flower. This is the habitat of the redstart, the wood-warbler and pied flycatcher. The otter also survives in these tranquil glades.

The area has been little disturbed by man. Ancient villages established by the Anglo-Saxons, places like Eggleston, Dufton, Hilton, Murton, are an integral part of the landscape beauty. Some are green villages, evolving slowly around the heart of a village green and surrounded by open fields.

Since the decline of lead-mining in the nineteenth century the population has been falling. Today, with twenty-five people to the square mile compared with the national average of 362 per square mile, the North Pennines have one of the lowest densities of inhabitants for any place of comparable size in England.

On 12 September 1986, after a twenty-day public inquiry, the Government confirmed the designation of the North Pennines as an Area of Outstanding Natural Beauty, eight years after the proposal to designate it was first made by the Countryside Commission. The new status enjoyed by the region does not mean that it is now immune from damage by building, mining or new farming practises, but it does oblige local authorities, government departments and other official bodies to give careful thought to the effect upon this outstanding landscape when they consider any proposed development within its boundaries.

OPPOSITE, ABOVE *New fencing at Bollihope Common near Middleton*
OPPOSITE, BELOW *The High Force, the highest waterfall in Britain*

Farmer at Middleton in Teesdale

Children playing in the tributary of the river Derwent at Blanchland

The West Midlands

Michael Westmoreland HAS DEVELOPED A FASCINATING TECHNIQUE OF PANORAMIC PHOTOGRAPHY THAT IS PARTICULARLY APPROPRIATE FOR THE ENGLISH LANDSCAPE · HE HAS EXHIBITED IN LONDON ON A NUMBER OF OCCASIONS AT THE PHOTOGRAPHERS GALLERY AND ELSEWHERE, AND HAS GREAT FEELING FOR THE COUNTRYSIDE

On a gentle rise in rolling Northamptonshire farmland, England divides. To the east two small streams slip away on a progress to merge their waters with the river Nene, which will eventually spill into the gaping mouth of East Anglia, the Wash. To the west there is a trickle, which swells into a stream, which becomes the principal among the many rivers in England known as the Avon. Below Stratford-upon-Avon it joins the Severn and drains into the Bristol Channel on Britain's western shore.

There was another watershed here on this ridge above Naseby, between Northampton and Market Harborough; it was the decisive event in one of Britain's most bitter internal conflicts. North of the village on some of the highest ground in the county, between Broad Moor and Fenny Hill, is the presumed site of the Battle of Naseby in 1645. Fairfax, the commander of Oliver Cromwell's New Model Army in the Civil War between Parliament and the King, won a resounding victory over the Royalists, led by Prince Rupert. An obelisk, away from the battle site, records a moral: 'The battle led to the subversion of the throne, the altar and the constitution ... leaving a useful lesson to British kings not to exceed the bounds of their prerogative.'

This is one of the least spoilt of England's Civil War battlefields. The landscape, farmed and improved but never built upon in over 300 years, offers no clues. The effort of recreating this famous contest lies in the imagination of the visitor, beholding this undulating vista.

Joined at ten in the morning of 14 June 1645, the battle was over by noon. The Royalists were resoundingly beaten despite an opening charge by Prince Rupert which carried all before him. This was the most important battle of the Civil War: within the year the War was over. Charles I was arrested in 1647 by the Parliamentarians at Holdenby in Northamptonshire and later executed.

This small but momentous fight left not a mark on its environment. There may be a relic of those June days in the church at Naseby: it contains a secular feature – a large plain table. One story has it that Cromwell dined off it the night after his victory; another has the King's Life Guards taking their meal on it the night before the battle.

Nothing much has touched any of this quiet landscape in the north of Northamptonshire, away from the industrial engine of this small county around Northampton and Kettering. Neat communities are spaced at random, built in the local limestone, which comes in a range of hues from creamy white to dark orange.

The county sits astride the belt of oolite limestone which begins around Portland Bill in Dorset and runs through the centre of England, through the Cotswolds and continuing to the Cleveland Hills in north-east England. These Northamptonshire villages are built in much the same rich stone, and they have an attractive uniformity.

Stanford on Avon, a village seven miles north-east of Rugby, revolves around the impressive church of St Nicholas, placed on a rise in the ground at the crossroads of the village. Most of its architecture dates from the early 1300s. It is built in a splendidly haphazard mix of pink limestone and brown ironstone, with fine chancel windows containing some of the finest stained glass in the country. Inside, among a collection of ornate tombs, is an extravagant curiosity, a life-size statue of a grieving hussar in full uniform.

This is in the broad, flat, well-hedged valley of the river Avon. On its eastern side is the Grand Union Canal, once a vital artery for industry, today a placid waterway for recreation. It clings to the lowest contours of the base of the Hemplow Hills which rise to the east. These hills are not a well-promoted beauty spot, but from this unsung place there is a view as perfect in its restrained rural beauty as any, a long sweeping panorama of rolling countryside in undeveloped England.

The Department of Transport's preferred route for the new link road between the M1 motorway and the A1 trunk-road, forty miles to the east, would cut across the unspoilt rural northern part of Northamptonshire, from the M1's junction with the M6 at Catthorpe, across the valley of the Avon, close to Stanford, past the Hemplow Hills, and close to the site of the battlefield of Naseby. CPRE has pressed consistently for an alternative, if marginally longer, route, which would not damage so much splendid countryside.

Treeline bordering the Grand Union Canal. The proposed route of the new link-road is just behind this line

The tranquil Hemplow Hills

The Grand Union Canal, with the Hemplow Hills in the distance. The proposed link-road would bridge the canal within yards of this point

BELOW AND PAGES 166 TO 168 *Cornfield vista between Stanford on Avon and Claycoton looking east towards the Hemplow Hills along the line of the proposed road*

Postscript

Vanishing England is not simply a book of photographs. It is a record of the continuing struggle to save our beautiful countryside, led by the Council for the Protection of Rural England – CPRE for short.

CPRE is the leading independent group in Britain campaigning for the conservation of our countryside. It is a membership body, with an unparalleled record of success and effectiveness in mobilising public opinion in the fight for this rural heritage.

Founded in 1926, and operating as a charity, free from any financial or political affiliation, CPRE was set up originally to fight for order in the chaotic pattern of ribbon development which threatened much of England's countryside in the 1920s and 1930s. The success of these early endeavours struck a chord with many people and CPRE's influence grew steadily.

Today, with over 30,000 members in forty-three branches up and down the country, CPRE is a more effective watchdog than ever, at a time when our natural heritage faces increasing threats from powerful pressures of many kinds. Heading active groups of ordinary people at local *and* national levels are CPRE's President, film producer David Puttnam, and its Chairman, David Astor.

CPRE's headquarters are in Westminster, London, where it has an expert campaign staff in constant contact with MPs, Government Ministers, Whitehall officials and the news media. Each of the forty-three county branches has its own chairman, secretary, committees and members, active in the defence of their own local countryside. Collectively, CPRE's efforts can show many achievements: the Green Belts, which prevent urban sprawl and ensure greening and open land around our cities; the modern planning system, which helps protect the rural environment through the Town and Country Planning Acts; and the

National Parks which were created to safeguard some of our wildest and most beautiful scenery. CPRE played a key role in the creation of all of these.

CPRE's principal weapons have always been sound research, persistence and the power of public opinion, reflected in a membership and staff tireless in the defence of the rural heritage. Literally thousands of battles have been fought by CPRE all over the country, to protect local landscapes. Some, like the Norfolk Broads, the New Forest and the Somerset Levels, are internationally renowned. Others are simply the precious village greens of rural England. There is still much to be done – and little sign today that the threats to our countryside have abated in any way.

The photographs featured in *Vanishing England* were taken for CPRE in 1985 and 1986 to mark its Diamond Jubilee, as a survey of threatened England. Through the medium of photography, it aimed to bring home what is now at stake in the struggle to protect the landscape from a growing range of threats and pressures. Each area shown faces a serious and imminent possibility of destruction or change. The photography provides a simple demonstration of what is under threat and of how every section of the English countryside is now affected.

The generosity and commitment of the photographers to CPRE's broad aims has been remarkable. Most of them gave their time free of charge, as it would have been impossible for CPRE to have financed such an ambitious project on its own. The resulting work, which went on show at the Royal Festival Hall in the Autumn of 1986, made up one of the most spectacular photographic exhibitions ever seen in Britain. The exhibition was called *Tomorrow*, because the *future* of the countryside is CPRE's key concern. The beauty of rural England is not ours to destroy; it belongs to our children and to future generations.

CPRE – a growing and effective campaigning force – needs *your* positive support and involvement. It is an independent body, whose effectiveness rests on the backing of members and supporters. The threatened landscapes shown in this book are only one part of a continuing story. You can help CPRE fight for *your* heritage now – by sending a donation to David Puttnam CBE, President, CPRE, Vanishing Landscapes, 4 Hobart Place, London, SW1W 0HY.

George Weidenfeld and Nicolson Ltd
91 Clapham High Street, London sw4 7ta

First published in the United States by Salem House Publishers, 1987,
462 Boston Street, Topsfield, ma 01983.

Library of Congress Catalog Card Number: 86-63308

isbn: 0 88162 247 8